DESTINY PURSUERS

Discovering Your Divine Purpose

Andrew Mutana

DEDICATION

This book is dedicated to The Almighty God our Heavenly Father and all the incessant pursuers of destiny.

Acknowledgements

First and foremost, I like to express my heartfelt gratitude to the Almighty God – my Father and my Friend. Thank You for carrying me through life!

It is my priviledge to share my life as well as my perspective about life with you (my readers).

The one person who was used by God to shape my life was my late mother – Eriosi Ruth Nantege. I pray every day that God will help me live up to the example she demonstrated and the legacy she left behind for us.

I also thank God for my wife, Deborah and our children. You are part of my life and spiritual journey. No words can express my gratitude to you as you journey with me.

I'm also greatly indebted to the several partners and friends from all over the world. I just can't mention all of you on this page. Thank you for making it possible for us to fulfill our destiny in God.

I also acknowledge the editing work done by my friend Pastor Alicia Teo of Trinity Community Center, Singapore and help in publishing this edition.

Impact Church, you are amazing! I'm grateful to God for all the staff and the members. Thank you for believing in us.

Finally, there are also countless authors, writers and pastors who have shaped my destiny.

Thank you. Without your contribution, this book would not have been written.

Andrew Mutana

TABLE OF CONTENTS

Andrew Mutana

INTRODUCTION

As young children in school, we were often told of 'the bright future ahead of us.' I often imagined – even fantasized on what this bright future would look like.

However, as we all know, the future is not an abstract, ambiguous or detached event. It is created in small bits – through the daily decisions and choices we make. God remains in control of all unknowns that is to come. We cannot fathom His mysteries. He is full of surprises way beyond our comprehension. (Jeremiah 29:11). But to a certain extent He has called us to participate with Him in this journey of shaping our destiny to His original intention.

Perfect conditions?

Most people may think that, in order for that future to be attained, all conditions have to be perfect. If that was the case, then I would not stand a chance.

I was raised in what many today call "a dysfunctional family." I am the eldest of 4 boys – born to the same mother having different fathers. Our fathers were all absent – a fact that we never quite understood as young children. I personally never got to know who my father was till I was 20 years of age. As a young boy, I suffered abuse and rejection. I even contemplated suicide when I was only 8!

We are a product of what we've been through – our background, environment, experiences and struggles. The way we turn out largely depends on our response to our life experiences in the past. We can end up as what many have called victims of circumstances— barely making it through life or victors over circumstances—using the unfortunate experiences we've been through as a stepping stone to higher ground.

My purpose of writing this Book is to encourage all the fatherless and those who are going through desert experience that you do not need to be a victim of defeat but a student of destiny as you journey with me in this Book. I believe God has a message and plan for you. It is by divine purpose that you have picked up this Book.

The destiny journey

The whole journey to Destiny starts with knowing we are (Identity) and what we were created to be (Purpose). Knowing our true identity and purpose is so important in our life. The first few chapters will be focused on both identity and purpose.

To have a clear understanding of both identity and purpose, we have to connect to God (our Creator) through prayer. Furthermore, we must learn to pray in order to obtain strength to continue this journey. Life can be tough! Often times, we have to deal with the unexpected. During such times, unless we pray, we will succumb to the temptation to give up – throw in the towel or lower our standard is greatest. We will look at the power of prayer that moves us forward to be an overcomer. (Romans 8:37)

Once we discover our purpose, we begin the process of unlocking our potential. The journey of living to the fullness of our potential can be long and arduous.

Passion is the drive which sustains and enables us to keep pursuing this purpose even in difficult times. We shall delve into the connection between the purpose, potential, price, pain, passion and power which we will cover in several chapters.

Finally, to achieve our purpose we need provision of resources. The primary resource, are the people whom God ordains to be part of our lives, to help us on our journey. Secondly, we need financial or material provision.

Interestingly, as you browse through this book, you will see that financial resources should be the least of our worries. You and I should instead embrace our purpose in Christ Jesus. Once we pursue His Kingdom, we will not have to pursue provision. It overtakes us.

Essentially, this book will take you through 8 P's – Prayer, Purpose, Potential, Price, Pain, Passion, Power and Provision. In my opinion, prayer is the pivot – the center – around which all the other 7 P's rotate and function. Only through prayer can we obtain the power that keeps us on course even when the price for destiny takes us through pain.

Purpose of this book

In my early years there was a time when deep in my spirit, I got tired of the mundane – living an average life. I decided that I was going to live by faith. I would believe every promise that God had given in His Word. I would live to the fullness of what God intended for me. This journey of faith, I must say, is not for the faint hearted. It calls for total reliance on God's power.

Have I arrived yet? No! Not yet! In fact, I still have a long way to go. I can agree with Paul's statement, "I do not consider myself yet to have taken hold of it. But one thing I do*Forgetting what is behind and straining toward what is ahead"* (Philippians 3:13).

What I've penned down in this book comes from several years of teaching, mentoring and counseling.

My prayer for you as you read this book is that you get revelation that will change your life. I pray that you will not simply read this Book for information. Hopefully, you'll receive revelation from the lessons I pen in this Book which may be applicable in your life to bring you to the next level.

May God nudge you out of your comfort zone and move you to greater heights!

CHAPTER 1

WHO ARE YOU?

Three main questions every person asks himself or herself are:

1.   Who am I? – Identity

2.   What am I here for? – Purpose

3.   What will my future look like? – Destiny

I was confronted with these questions at a very young age. Through my struggles, pain and challenges, I have found some answers. I will endeavor to share with you the answers to these questions in the best way I possibly can.

Who are you?

This is a pertinent question because without a proper appreciation of who you are; you can never live to realize both your purpose and potential or reach your destiny.

From the onset, it is important for you to understand that the answer to this question is none of these below:

•   What you do

•   What race or colour you are

•   What certificate or title you hold

My struggle with being fatherless

The importance of a father in the life of a child cannot be overstated. I perfectly empathize with the growing number of fatherless children in our world today.

Growing up, as a young boy without a father, almost completely destroyed me. As I said earlier, mom raised us as a single mother. I must say that she was a hardworking woman. And I give her credit for all she did. But she could only do that much. With her meagre wages, she often struggled to meet the very basic of our needs.

Life was tough and rough. I often joke that even the poor people called us poor! Even harder was the fact that I felt unwanted. I had learned, as a little boy, that when I was born, my father had refused to acknowledge me as his child. Due to this thought, I often wrestled with feelings of rejection, hopelessness and worthlessness.

Identity crisis

My biggest struggle, as I later found out was the search for identity. I deeply needed to know that I was loved and accepted. The reason I had battled with low self-esteem and rejection was because of the information I had been fed with.

This information had blurred my view of life, people and even God. It was very difficult for me to relate to God. I just could not imagine that God, our Heavenly Father could love me or even have a plan for me. To me this was mind-boggling.

Our world is full of restless people. This restlessness can be captured by some of the catchwords or phrases used by this generation. I'm sure you've heard people say, "I really need a personal makeover." Or you may heard someone say, "I need to redefine or reinvent myself!"

Though this is not a new problem, it has been aggravated in our days because of easier access to media. With the advent of social media, we are constantly checking on how many likes, views or followers we have. As people watch T.V., surf the Internet or read books and magazines, they try to live up to the lifestyle of some of the actors, actresses and models. That quest of trying to be the person we admire, robs us of the joy of living a fulfilled life.

There is really nothing wrong with attempting to look or live better. The problem is that most of these endeavours are driven by comparisons and competition. People are often driven by an inferiority complex (negative feelings of low self-esteem) because of desiring to be like somebody else they admire.

Remember, we are all unique. We are not carbon copies. We are originals and uniquely formed by God and He has a unique plan for each one of us. (Psalm 139:13-16)

Where are the fathers?

God spoke through the ancient prophet Malachi;

"And he shall turn the heart of the fathers to the children, and the heart of the children to their fathers, lest I come and smite the earth with a curse."(Malachi 4:6)

Perhaps you like to reflect on what the Prophet is saying. Why would God smite the earth with a curse because of an issue unless that issue was very grievous and not good for us? That curse, in my opinion is this identity crisis our generation faces today mostly caused by the absence of fathers.

This identity crisis affects all ages but mostly the younger people. In fact, most of us seem to be alright until we join school. In my childhood years, I didn't know there was anything wrong with me or my family until I joined school. Young boys and girls are normally expressive with their thoughts. Some children started asking me all sorts of questions that made me uncomfortable.

Most parents shower their children with unconditional love. Fathers in particular offer a sense of security and affirmation to their children. Those who lack a safe home environment struggle with trusting others. This causes them to normally pass sarcastic remarks and at times hurting remarks. Some of them even make you feel or look bad so they can feel better about themselves. Others do it because they want you to be part of their clique or gang. Sadly, driven by the desire to be accepted in the clique – to fit in, most young people are willing to compromise their standards.

Bastard! – A new word to me

Mom worked at a small clinic belonging to one of our relatives. We also lived in their home probably because we couldn't afford renting a house. Our relatives were nice kindhearted people. However, there were more than 10 other people inhabiting with this family.

My naive expectation as a child is what caused me to get hurt. I thought that I deserved to be treated like my cousins. Obviously, I wasn't.

Often times, I tried to demand my 'rights' in vain. This often left me very angry and frustrated especially when provoked. It was probably due to this vent up frustration, I became a violent little boy. I had frequent outbursts of anger.

I found out later that this attitude was due to a desire to seek attention. I recall that when I was around 8, I got into a fight with one of my cousins. She blurted out, "You are a bastard, son of a woman..." "Bastard" was a new word to me. I really didn't know what it meant, so I sought to find out.

When I discovered, I was so disturbed in my spirit. Satan really used that word to rock my world. I went through a severe depression. I could hear all these voices telling me, "No one really loves you. No one cares. You have no future..." I would sit by myself and cry for hours. It got so bad that at some point I was distraught and lost my vision, finding no meaning in life. Young as I was, I contemplated suicide.

The turning point

This 'hitting-the-rock-bottom' situation was the turning point for my life. I came across a little book that God used to minister to me. That little book written by Dr. T. L Osborn was entitled, "You are God's best." The book had deliberate statements like; "You are not a mistake; you are not a second hand; you were created to do something unique that no one else can ever accomplish if you don't..."

Just about the same time, my brother who had been born with a heart condition was miraculously healed by the power of God. That miracle became the catalyst for my mother's salvation. She took us to her new church home – a small Full Gospel church in town. A few years later, at the altar of that church, I surrendered my life to Christ. For the first time, there was a deep sense of knowing that my life counted for something. In retrospect, it is clear to me that God orchestrated all these events.

Everybody has a story

As you can see, I struggled with an identity crisis at a very tender age. I also hated myself. I often wished I was somebody else. I had an inferiority complex. Now I know why I used to feel this way. When I was born, my father rejected me. Seeds of rejection were sown in my young heart. I never thought I was good enough to be loved and appreciated by anybody. Even though my mother showered me with extravagant love.

Often, I would think I was facing these struggles alone. However, as I grew older, I began to realize that many people had similar struggles. And this is regardless of how much money one makes, how successful they are, how intelligent or beautiful they may be. Almost everyone goes through similar experiences at some point in their lives. Suffice to say, everybody has a story.

What's your story?

As we live through life and face difficult situations, we ask the hard questions:

- Why am I here?

- Why have I gone through all this?

- Is there anything more to life than this?

Do you remember a time when you felt awkward? Perhaps that was when you checked yourself in the mirror and noticed this one physical feature you wished wasn't part of your body. Or when you met someone who made a comment that reminded you of some shameful experience in the past.

Most of the times we feel so inadequate in comparison with another person's ability, beauty, personality, charisma or achievements. Such are moments of discouragement, depression and hopelessness. They reveal our vulnerability and imperfections as human beings.

To live a meaningful, purposeful life we must confront these realities. We must not bury our head in the sand and hope we'll feel better. We must honestly and truthfully find the answers to these questions, which are the roots of our current problems.

Andrew Mutana

Chapter 2

The Lies and the Truth

One day Jesus asked his twelve disciples whether they also wanted to leave Him like the rest of the disciples. Peter's reply makes the best introduction to this chapter. He answered, "To whom shall we go? You have the words of life." (John 6:68)

Words! They make us or destroy us. Certainly at that stage of his life, Peter had heard many words spoken to him. He recognized that Jesus' words were different – they imparted life. Not only was Jesus speaking truth. He is the Truth. So if what He spoke imparted life, we can conclude that lies impart death.

In my book on 'Spiritual warfare', we examine Satan's two effective weapons; "fear and lies". Unfortunately, human nature finds it easier to believe lies than to accept the truth.

In this chapter we will look at some of the lies most people end up believing. We can only confront these lies with the truth out of God's word.

What lies have you believed about yourself? I wonder!

Lie #1: I am a mistake

There are several people who think or have been made to believe that their birth was unplanned for – a mistake. Some of these people were born out of wedlock. It is not surprising that someone born out of wedlock should struggle with such a thought. This struggle often stems out from a feeling that one is rejected, unwanted, neglected or ostracized.

I personally struggled with such thoughts for a long time. I recall seeing children being picked up or dropped by their dads at school. I silently wondered where mine was. The biggest challenge was that my mother could react angrily whenever I asked her that question. I learned not to ask.

Others might have been told by their parents that their birth was not planned. I also know people who struggle with such thoughts because they were adopted by another family. However nice their adoptive parents may be, most adoptees just can't come to terms with the fact that their birthparents gave them up for adoption.

Even those who came out of great families do struggle with such thoughts. Often times, it may be because their parents treated them differently. Perhaps they wrongfully compared them to other siblings in their hearing. They could have struggled with the fact that they were not as good as…as smart as… as pretty as…the other sibling(s). Or because they failed to live to the expectations of the family, they were branded the 'black sheep' of the family.

Obviously, thinking that way leads to several negative traits in people's lives:

•   Low self-esteem

•   Throwing caution to the wind – living destructive lifestyles and resorting to all kinds of addictions just to numb the pain inside of them

- Self-pity

- Depression: You remember I shared earlier about my personal experience. I was depressed because of what I experienced as a child. I heard disturbing voices in my mind. Actually these were self-destructive talks as a result of the trauma of the word 'bastard'.

- Feelings of worthlessness – often causing one to become suicidal.

The truth: You were created by a loving Father

I listened to an interesting song many years back. These were some of the lyrics;

Preachers make mistakes

Doctors make mistakes

Parents make mistakes

But one thing my God can never do

He can never make a mistake

You are not a mistake!

You are not a product of evolution either.

You were created.

Your life was planned. Your life was carefully designed by God. He knew you and shaped you.

Your parents were simply the instrument He used to bring you to this earth. It doesn't really matter whether or not they planned to have you. What matters is that God planned your life. He loves and cares for you.

This is what the Bible says;

So God created man in his own image, in the image of God created he him; male and female created he them (Genesis 1:27)

The above scripture shows us that God was intentional. He chose to create human beings in His image. I don't know about you but I find this to be reassuring—the knowledge that I have a loving Heavenly Father. Not only did He create me; He has a wonderful plan for me. I am designed for success.

Lie #2: I am not good enough

The world often uses our differences to wrongly classify people. Differences in race, color, tribe, status, nationality, education... When I visited India, I was shocked to learn of their caste system. It almost advocates for treatment of certain human beings as animals.

It's strange but so true. We are always classified into things that we even don't know. Simply because we were born black or white or Asian, we are told that we belong somewhere. Sometimes it is because of socio-economic and geographical factors. Once you say that I am from Africa, for example, everyone thinks you are holding a begging bowl. If you happen to be applying for a visa at an embassy, you are immediately seen as a potential illegal immigrant.

It is these kinds of prejudices that make us all feel like second-class citizens. We silently wish we had a different skin color, another background or were born in another country. Perhaps then we would avoid the ignominy of profiling.

I cannot count how many women I have met who unfortunately believe the lie of the enemy that they are ugly. The irony always is that these are usually very beautiful women. However, somehow they got to believe these words about themselves. Most likely, whoever said it to them, was probably that someone who was jealous of their looks or one who was not successful in trying to become their friend.

Sadly, verbal abuse sometimes is from people we love and trust – our spouses, parents and friends. For parents, it is those times, when we make careless comparisons between our children. This makes one child feel that because he/she is not as smart or talented as the other sibling, they are not good enough.

Truth: You are fearfully and wonderfully made

Our God is a God of diversity. He made all of us unique and different. One of the most powerful passages in the Bible is Psalm 139.

A couple of years back, I was called to minister to a young lady who had attempted suicide. She was lying on a hospital bed having lost a lot of blood after slitting her wrist. By the grace of God, I shared the Gospel with this lady and she gave her life to Christ.

I met her several times before I left that country. In those discipleship sessions, I felt led by the Lord to ask her to continually read and meditate on this Psalm. After a number of times, I could tell that God was using these words to minister to her extensively.

The whole Psalm is so powerful but it is good to highlight verses 13-18.

For you created my inmost being;

> you knit me together in my mother's womb.

I praise you because I am fearfully and wonderfully made;

> *your works are wonderful,*
>
> *I know that full well.*

My frame was not hidden from you

> *when I was made in the secret place,*
>
> *when I was woven together in the depths of the earth.*

Your eyes saw my unformed body;

> *all the days ordained for me were written in your book*
>
> *before one of them came to be.*
>
> *How precious to me are your thoughts, God!*
>
> *How vast is the sum of them!*
>
> *Were I to count them,*
>
> *they would outnumber the grains of sand—*
>
> *when I awake, I am still with you.*

Lie #3: I have no future

We have all attempted certain things and failed. Perhaps, you tried out music, a certain kind of sports or tried to obtain a certain academic grade in vain. How we respond to failure at any stage of our lives determines a lot. If we do not respond correctly, we might think that our lives are doomed because we failed in a certain area.

The truth: You have a great future ahead

God is the Alpha and the Omega-meaning He is the first and the last. He told Moses that His name is the 'I AM.' When nothing else was He was. He declares the end from the beginning.

Just like an architect who plans the structure of a building, He designed our destiny even before we were born.

As Jeremiah 29:11 puts it, He alone knows the plans that He has for us. They are plans for prosperity and not disaster. They lead us to an expected end. Your expectation for good matters!

Sometime back, I heard Dr. Myles Munroe says that "God is committed to bring our future into our present and make it our past."

Lie #4: I am what the world has labeled me

Society tries to define us. As we grow into adulthood, we are influenced by culture, our families and environment. Oftentimes, we try to fit into this mould. We want to behave in a way acceptable to the people around us and we attempt to meet the expectations of our family or the community.

This is probably easier if that expectation or definition is good. However, the problem is that when we make mistakes, people tend to label us by those mistakes. What do you do when what people have defined you is something depressing, brings shame, guilt and terrible memories?

The truth: You are not what the world has labeled you

Your destiny is too important to be left to another man's hands.

It is all a matter of choice! You can choose to wallow in regret, throw a pity party or:

1. You can shed off every prejudice or label that the world has put on you.

2. You can choose to believe that no one has a right to define you. Not even your parents! They have no idea what God wants to do with your life.

3. And you can refuse to be intimidated, controlled or manipulated into being something else other than being who God formed you to be.

As we saw in Jeremiah 29:11, God alone knows the plans for your life. You are who God says you are. God always means good for you and watches over your life.

Lie #5: My present state defines or is a pointer to my destiny

Most of us may presently be in circumstances totally contradicting the vision we have of our destiny. We can easily lose hope if we fail to see the bigger picture.

Of course, today matters. We contribute to our destiny by the decisions and choices we make on a daily basis. What I'm talking about is a preoccupation with the past or the feeling of being overwhelmed with the magnitude of present difficulties we are facing.

The truth: Your present state doesn't define you

Looking at the text in Genesis 1, we see that the Spirit of God was hovering over a shapeless, confused and disorganized state of affairs. And right in the midst of what was happening, God spoke light into existence. This marked the beginning of creation.

In the same way, just as in the beginning, perhaps our lives and what we see around us could best be described as a shapeless, confused and disorganized state of affairs.

The God, who spoke light into darkness, wants to bring light in the dark places of your life. He wants to give you a new name and a new identity. But you must cooperate with him. You must acknowledge that you need His intervention in your life by surrendering your life to His Lordship today.

You can ask Jesus into your life by praying;

Lord Jesus, forgive me of my sins

Come into my heart and change me

I commit my life to you today

Be my Lord and my Savior

In Your precious Name I pray, Amen

Andrew Mutana

Part I

Prayer

"Prayer is the pivot that links passion, power, potential and provision. Only prayer will help us to stand when we have to pay the price or suffer pain and loss. Basically, we obtain power by receiving a Word from God. So, while it is good for us to talk to God, prayer really becomes powerful when God speaks."

Andrew Mutana

Andrew Mutana

CHAPTER 3

THE GOD CONNECTION

I said, Days should speak, and multitude of years should teach wisdom.

But there is a spirit in man: and the inspiration of the Almighty giveth them understanding.

Job 32:7-8,

From this scripture in the book of Job, two things are clear:

• God created us with a spirit. In fact, we are spirits having a soul, living in a body.

• We gain understanding through God's inspiration. That is, when our human spirit connects to His Spirit.

This connection is by and through prayer. Prayer simply defined is communication with God.

John Wesley said, "God does nothing apart from prayer and everything through it".

Therefore, it is of utmost importance for us to learn how to communicate with Him.

Creating an atmosphere for the Spirit to move

To understand this better, let's read Genesis 1:1-3.

In the beginning God created the heaven and the earth

And the earth was without form, and void; and darkness was upon the face of the deep. And the spirit of God moved upon the face of the waters.

And God said, Let there be light: and there was light.

This is an interesting verse. We will use it as the running theme in this book. Primarily, because of two reasons:

1.   It describes how God created the entire world from nothing. This is in our interest because most of us begin from zero – nothing – in our pursuit of destiny.

2.   This passage also describes the process of moving from nothing to something – the process of creation.

The state of the earth at the time of creation was dismal. It was void or empty and darkness covered the face of the deep. Everything seemed negative.

What actually stands out here is that the Spirit of God moved over the face of the waters. God's Spirit was moving over a disorganized, shapeless and empty state. The word 'moving' here is also translated as "hovering or brooding." I like the word 'brooding' better because in a metaphoric way, it shows how God's Spirit enveloped the earth in the same way mother hen sits over her un-hatched eggs.

As this happened, God said, "Let there be light…"

To summarize, three things are clear in this passage:

1. We understand that God works with a purpose in mind. In the beginning, that purpose was to create the heavens and the earth thereby bringing order to the existing confusion.

2. For creation to take place, a suitable atmosphere existed. This atmosphere – the Spirit of God moving (brooding, hovering) over the face of the waters enabled God to speak His Word to the situation. God spoke the entire world into existence.

3. This word was pregnant with "potential". The root of the word "potential" is potent which means something strong and powerful. In other words, the Word was filled with hidden or latent power. This power emanating from the spoken word generated the entire creation process.

Applying this to our pursuit of purpose, we can say that when we pray, five things happen

1. We create an atmosphere for the Spirit of God

2. God hovers or broods over our lives and our situations.

3. God speaks into our nothingness, emptiness and shapelessness.

4. His spoken Word or the seed of God is implanted in us in the same way a baby is conceived in the womb of a woman. It can be in the form of a dream, idea, vision or a verbal word of prophecy.

5. That word generates faith since faith comes by hearing the word (Romans 10:17).

It is from this scripture that I derive my definition of prayer as: *Creating an atmosphere for God to speak a creative word into our lives.*

Andrew Mutana

CHAPTER 4

PRAYER AND YOUR DIVINE DESTINY

There are many books out there on purpose, passion and destiny. Most of them are good self-help books. Some of them are written by well-meaning Christians. The only problem is that more than 80% of the ones I've read mostly give principles or formulas one can use to discover or determine their purpose.

This to me is a flawed process from the start. Why do I say so?

- Our ability as human beings to determine our own destiny is futile. Only the creator knows the reason why He created what He created.

- We all face setbacks on our journey as a result of which we realise that sheer will-power and tenacity aren't just enough to keep us going. That is why prayer is pivotal. Prayer is the pivot that links passion, power, potential and provision.

- Only prayer will help us to stand when we have to pay the price or suffer pain and loss.

Basically we obtain power by receiving a word from God. So, while it is good for us to talk to God, prayer really becomes powerful when God speaks. God's Word is a lamp. It lights our path. It helps us to see the unseen world.

I used the table below recently to illustrate the difference between living by information and living by revelation.

Information	Revelation
Comes by five natural senses	Comes through the Spirit of God
Causes fear and limitation	Causes faith
Walk by sight	Walk by faith
Only depends on hindsight	Brings clarity to hindsight. Is also the source of insight and foresight
False identity	Authentic identity

Prayer helps us break out of the barrier of dependence on sight (dependence on our natural senses) to walking by faith (revelation).

Faith is necessary to fulfill our divine purpose. We know that God created the world by His Word. Likewise, we create when we speak His Word into our world. Remember, creation is different from invention. By creating we are bringing to this Earth something that has never existed.

That's why you're here my friend. Through your uniqueness, God wants to touch the world in a way He never has through any other person.

However, for Him to do this you and I must cooperate with Him. And the first thing we need to do is discover our purpose. What were we created to do?

As we conclude this chapter, let's look at some key points:

1. He is the source of our dreams and it is only as we wait on Him that He keeps revealing how He wants them accomplished.

2. We need to spend more time with God – more than we spend trying to win the favour of men. Along the way we will need people – key people to help us achieve our destiny. Joseph needed the butler in his path – for him to get access to Pharaoh's palace. As we pray, God will put in our path the divine connections we need to reach our destiny.

3. When connections are divine, God maintains them. When they are born out of our fleshly maneuvers, we struggle to maintain them in vain.

4. As we fellowship with Him, we become authentic and original.

5. As we pray God will lead us to His destiny for our lives.

6. We'll gain power to accomplish what God has called us to do

Andrew Mutana

CHAPTER 5

WAITING FOR THE VISION

I learned recently that most car headlights only give the drivers visibility of up to 200m at night. Our life is designed like that. While our destiny may be 300km from where we presently are, we will have to fulfill the '200m vision' first before getting to the next place. Of course some of the 200m visions will be intertwined.

Vision is simply what we see. Without the vision, it is impossible for us to see the way forward. God wants us to see with eyes of faith – beyond what is visible to the physical eye. And that is only possible through prayer.

Perhaps the most vivid connection between prayer and vision is the scripture in Habakkuk 2:1-4.

I will stand upon my watch, and set me upon the tower, and will watch to see what he will say unto me, and what I shall answer when I am reproved.

And the LORD answered me, and said, Write the vision, and make it plain upon tables, that he may run that readeth it.

For the vision is yet for an appointed time, but at the end it shall speak, and not lie: because it will surely come, it will not tarry.

Behold, his soul which is lifted up is not upright in him: but the just shall live by his faith.

God spoke to Habakkuk about the vision. He was told that he had to stand upon the watch and wait to see what He would say.

Before we proceed, I must point out two lessons from the life of Habbakuk:

- He had a place (his watch) - an altar. This was where he waited on God.

- He was not told to *wait and hear* what God would say. Rather, he was told to *wait and see.* This means that when God speaks, He creates a tangible thing that can be seen.

Friend, there is a difference between those who constantly wait in His presence to see what He will say and those who don't. Just as fish cannot survive outside water, we cannot make it outside His presence.

The secret place

Waiting must be deliberate – intentional. We have to set aside a time, a place to commune with Him. God is not a computer. We cannot just think of turning to Him in difficult times or crisis. We cannot use or manipulate Him. We must have an ongoing, unbroken relationship with Him. *It is he who dwells in the secret place of the Most High that abides under the shadow of the Almighty.* (Psalm 91:1-2)

Throughout scriptures we see this secret place. For Moses, it was the cleft of the rock. For Daniel, it was the window overlooking the city. For Jesus, it was nights at the mountaintop alone.

Summary

One morning, after about five hours of intense prayer, I fell on my bed feeling physically exhausted. I then had a vision in which I saw the whole sky filled with drawers facing down to the earth. As I thought about what I had seen, the Spirit of God spoke to me that there is so much that God desires to release to the earth. The problem is that no one is paying the price to bring it down; not many even know what is theirs.

For us to know, we have to 'breakthrough' in prayer. As an illustration, Moses' tabernacle was made of the outer court, the inner court and the holy of holies. The high priest in the Old Covenant was the only one who accessed into the Holy of Holies.

Today, God calls us to enter boldly into the throne of grace so that we can find mercy and obtain grace, to help in time of need. (Hebrews 4:14-16) We move beyond the outer court and the Holy Place through Praise and Worship. Then we get to the place when nothing hinders our communion. In His presence, like Moses, we can talk to Him as a man talks to a fellow man.

This grace we obtain is the power to accomplish His will – fulfill our purpose in the face of adversity and opposition. God's plan cannot be thwarted (Job 42:2).

God is ready. Are we?

We need the power of God now more than ever before. The world needs to see a demonstration of the power of God. In Ephesians 6, Paul used the word "wrestle" while referring to our fight with the powers of darkness. This means that to change the world, we must be willing to fight. We must pay the price of staying in His presence until

He changes everything around us.

Interestingly, Jesus said that all we need is faith as small as a mustard seed to speak to a mountain to move (Matthew 17:6, 20). The mustard seed metaphor is powerful.

Basically, this small mustard seed when planted and nurtured well, does become a large tree where birds from all nations find their shelter. This is how powerful that which is born of God can be.

The more we pray, the more we will have power to take healing and deliverance to the nations of the world.

So how do we move from creating the atmosphere, receiving the word of God – to actually seeing it come to pass? Hearing God's word is very exciting. We often see the amazing possibilities lying ahead.

However, it is important to be reminded that this is a process that will require waiting. Waiting is only possible by exercising the same faith we received as we obtained the Word from God over and over again.

What that means is that we have to pray – pray more – and more – until we see the fulfillment of the vision.

Part II

Potential

"You must decide if you are going to rob the world or bless it with the rich, valuable, potent, untapped resources locked away within you."

Myles Munroe, Understanding Your Potential

Andrew Mutana

CHAPTER 6

POTENTIAL

Y ou have just purchased a new product and you are very excited. It is probably a car, or music system or freezer. Finally your dream has come true. As you open the package, you come across a book. This book is the manual for that product. What we often see written on the first page of that book is this: You must read the instructions within this book carefully before operating the product.

We often don't want to spend time reading the manual. Speaking for myself, I don't remember when I last sat down to understand how the item I had just bought worked. When I buy a new item, I normally have the adrenaline rush of excitement running through my veins. I just can't wait to press those buttons.

What is really contained in the manual is the potential of the product. This potential is clearly related to the purpose this

product was designed to serve. While we often have a purpose in mind – the reason why we bought the item in the first place, most of us fail to unearth the full potential because we are either lazy or uninterested in the detail.

Using that analogy; God is the manufacturer and we are the product. He has written the Bible – the manual through which we can understand our potential.

Each one of us has greatness embedded in our spirit. That potential is the capacity built within us to handle and accomplish the purpose we were created for.

Inbuilt checks

Without the manufacturer's manual a product may be misused, abused or underutilized. In my study of Electrical Engineering, we undertook a unit called Control Systems Engineering. We were told that products have to be subjected to intense and strenuous conditions to test their ability before they are released to the market. Without this process, a product could end up functioning the exact opposite of what it was meant to do. Using equations, the prototype's performance is analyzed thoroughly. Then, it is put on the production line.

Therefore, the manufacturer knows that his product is capable to perform all the functions in the manual. If as human beings we can put in place such checks, then what about the Almighty God!

Abraham's seed

God spoke to our father Abraham in Genesis 22:17.

That in blessing I will bless thee, and in multiplying I will multiply thy seed as the stars of the heaven, and as the sand which is upon the seashore; and thy seed shall possess the gate of his enemies.

He told him that He would bless and multiply him. He told him that his seed would possess the gate of his enemies. Literary the seed talked of his descendants. Let me submit to you, that seed also represented the word or covenant God had with Abraham.

In other words, God was telling Abraham, "I have put within you the ability to possess the gates of your enemies."

Getting back to Genesis 1:3 as I had earlier explained, the Word that God spoke was a seed pregnant with all that He was creating. When He spoke light into the darkness, light was carried by the Word He had spoken. Interestingly, light was created and existed before the sun, the moon and stars were.

In the same way, God has already put within us all that you and I need to fulfill His purpose. When we hear His word like Abraham and act on it, we unlock that seed. Nobody is holding our opportunities, resources and treasures. You and I may not have it today. But God has already given us the power to attract it. God has placed within every living creature the ability to reproduce its own kind (Genesis 1:16).

There is power in a seed. A pine seed could yield one tree or it could end up becoming a forest. In other words: "Never underestimate the Power of a seed. The creative ability – multiplier effect within this one seed is what I call "Potential".

The word "Potential" has its root as the word "Potent" – power. No wonder, our God is called the Omnipotent God – the all-powerful God!

God created every creature with a seed to reproduce its kind.

Everything we need has already been placed in us as we have already seen. All we need, when we discover this potential, is to push it out of us. The process of pushing it out of our wombs is often a struggle – a fight – sometimes a matter of life and death!

CHAPTER 7

POTENTIAL INHIBITORS

W e will look at a number of things which can paralyse our potential, causing us to live below God's purpose.

1. Failure to know who you are

2. The Blame Game

3. Dwelling on the Past

Failure to know who you are

When the value of a product is not appreciated, that product is prone to abuse or misuse. In the same way, most of us do not really value the precious lives and gifts God has given us. As a result, we easily open ourselves to people who take advantage of us.

We accept to be defined according to people's opinions of us. Often times, we cry because we realize that people we trusted have used us, abused us, manipulated, controlled, suppressed and contained us. We can be angry at those people, yet oftentimes, there is a vulnerability we expose in our relationships that invites people to negatively affect us.

When we know who we are;

1. We are able to say "No" to things which do not lie within the parameters of our value system.

2. We are able to sacrifice instant gratification for later joy and happiness.

There are several examples in the Bible on this subject but none could be better than that of Esau and Jacob.

In Genesis 25:31-34 we read;

Jacob said, "Sell me your birthright now." 32 Esau said, "I am about to die; of what use is a birthright to me?" 33 Jacob said, "Swear to me now." So he swore to him and sold his birthright to Jacob. 34 Then Jacob gave Esau bread and lentil stew, and he ate and drank and rose and went his way. Thus Esau despised his birthright. (ESV)

How sad it is to see Esau despising his birthright! Yet we do it every day. How? You might ask yourself. The answer is: Through the choices and decisions we make.

The blame game

Some of the things we struggle with are consequences of our own bad decisions. However, often times we are faced with challenges that resulted from other people's actions. These may have been people God gave the responsibility to defend or provide for us. Yet the same people could have turned against us – probably even abusing us physically.

I was personally a victim of this. But I refused to live the rest of my life blaming my father for not being there; blaming my relatives for destroying my self-esteem as a child; or even blaming people who never came to my mother's help when they could have.

I dare you to stop the blame game. You see this whole blaming business started with Adam & Eve in Genesis 3. He blamed his wife Eve. Eve blamed the serpent. We spend most of our lifetime blaming other people for our predicament. We blame our upbringing, education, friends and even governments or politicians.

Break up the pity party and have a life. If your circumstances are a result of your sin; repent! God is full of grace and mercy. Accept His forgiveness, and move on.

If your predicament is a result of other people's mistakes, sin or negligence; forgive and release them. I know it's not easy. But it is much harder living the rest of your life, a captive of other people's poor choices and decisions. It is time to forgive others and forgive yourself. If you still have self-destructive talk within yourself, you have not forgiven yourself.

Dwelling on the past

We may not have chosen our past. We certainly never chose which home to be born in and to which parents. And as you read this Book, you may be reasoning within yourself that "This writer does not know what you have been through!" Of course I don't. I would not want you to think for a second that I'm trivializing your pain.

What I do know is this; our past affects us all to a certain degree. But we don't have to accept the devil's lie that we don't have what it takes to make it. We have to take full responsibility for our future.

Moreover, once we realize God's purpose for our lives, all these are insignificant.

Regardless of how terrible our past may be, we have hope that God has the best future in store for us.

CHAPTER 8

MAXIMIZING THE MOMENT

Let us look at what Solomon said in Ecclesiastes 9:11.

I returned, and saw under the sun, that the race is not to the swift, nor the battle to the strong, neither yet bread to the wise, nor yet riches to men of understanding, nor yet favour to men of skill; but time and chance happeneth to them all.

We all know that Solomon was the wisest man who ever lived. He was greater than all the other philosophers. He took time to study life and what makes it work. Much of that wisdom is collected in the Book of Proverbs and the Book of Ecclesiastes.

The text above is one of those discoveries. It contains four important truths:

• Success has no real formula – Everyone would think that the fastest man will always win the race or that hard work always pays. But that's not always the case.

• Anyone can make it. It is not the most endowed that always make it in life.

• There is a set time – also called the Kairos moment for everyone. Some people call it being in the right place at the right time. However, with God there are no coincidences. When we trust Him, we realize that He positions us to meet certain people.

• Everybody has a chance – we term it "God's grace" and favour."

Time and Chance

I have heard a cliché, which says, "Every dog has its day." There is so much power in understanding your time and season. Things may be going downhill today. Everybody may believe it is over with you. But as is written in the Bible, weeping may endure for a night but joy comes in the morning. (Psalm 30:5)

When the fullness of time comes, the potential begins to shine. I compare this to the seed, which has found a favourable soil. No matter what you do to a seed as long as it is not destroyed, it has the power to produce its kind. You may cover it with mud, kick it around or store it away. However, the day it gets the right conditions it will bud into a fresh plant. You never know how much that once despised seed will yield.

Chance talks of favour. The right time brings a divine favor that attracts things to you. When you operate in that favor, whatever you invest will prosper. People that you need will be easily connected to you. Favour can change a slave into royalty overnight. If you don't believe this, look at the story of Joseph or Esther in the Bible.

One day, Joseph is languishing in incarceration and the next he is ruling as a prince.

Esther spends a life in rejection, pain and oblivion. Favor before the king propels her to the greatest position of influence anyone could ever dream of. She was able to halt the plans of wicked Haman to save the Jewish nation from annihilation.

So how do we get it right? – Use your time and chance optimally?

1. We have to mature to a level of creating opportunity instead of waiting for it

It is amazing how many people in the developing countries think that migrating to the developed world would make them instantly successful. Many people sell their fortune to buy a ticket to fly to wherever they think their opportunity lies.

I'm aware certain areas have a certain potential because of the investments made over the years... What saddens me is the handout mentality that plagues some immigrants.

This same mentality sometimes grips the leaders of our governments – thinking that somebody, somewhere, owes us a handout or aid. Nothing could be further from the truth. What we need is lift up our hands not a hand-out.

Successful people create opportunities. They take what is ordinary and turn it into something extraordinary. . They don't wait for people to give them great opportunities.

As the late Archbishop Benson Idhahosa once said, "A lizard in Africa will still be a lizard in America".

2. We must start looking within for our success

For example, Africa is potentially the richest continent. It has all the resources the world is craving for - oil, gold, diamonds, and great tourism sites. It has the best soils and best climates all the year round. Our problem as Africans therefore, is not the lack of potential but the ability to harness it for our good.

On an individual level, we realize that it is hard work to become who we are supposed to be. One can die a pauper when God has invested within them great talents and skills that could make them immensely wealthy.

CHAPTER 9

DISCOVERING AND RELEASING POTENTIAL

How do we release this powerful force within us? First of all, we need to know our potential. We can only release what we are aware of.

Knowledge comes to us in two ways – by information and more so by revelation.

Information is what we obtain through the natural senses – hearing, seeing, tasting, touching and smelling. Here are some of the ways we acquire information:

- Our environment: This can give us leads to discovering our potential. By environment, I mean the people around us – family, schools we go to, church...

- Reading also opens our minds and helps us increase our capacity to conceptualize

- Training

- Exposure.

Information however is limited.

When Jesus asked His disciples who He was, only Peter correctly identified Him as the Messiah. Jesus told Peter that flesh and blood had not revealed this to him. This had been revealed by the Father in heaven. Peter was operating in a realm beyond information.

When we consider the replies of the other disciples it shows that they used the information that they had about Jesus. On this revelation Peter had about Jesus being the Son of God, Jesus said the church would be built and the gates of hell would not prevail against it. (Matthew 16:13-19). God's greater plan was the birth of the Church, which the disciples could not fathom.

Revelation only comes from God

Prayer is the only tool that the Creator has given us to communicate with Him. When we pray He begins to light the torch on the intrinsic wealth He has placed in us. Though people do help us identify our talents only the Creator can show us what He created us to do. Life is a continuous sanctification and transforming process. We are shaped by Him through to eternity.

In Jeremiah 33:3, God tells us;

Call to Me and I will answer you and show you great and mighty things, fenced in and hidden, which you do not know (do not distinguish and recognise, have knowledge of and understand). Ampli ed Bible

David was one man who called on the Lord in his lifetime. In Psalm 16:11, He says;

You will show me the path of life; In Your presence is fullness of joy; At Your right hand are pleasures evermore.

He was confident of two things:

- God knew the path his life would take

- God would show him this path

David clearly knew his purpose in life. He also says in Psalms 40:7, *"Lo I come, in the volume of the book it is written of me"*

David believed that God had a book in which all of the days of our lives are written. I also do. So how do we access this information – written in the volume? It is by revelation.

Revelation also helps us to discern the timing and 'place' for the breakthrough. This place is where our seed will blossom and be fruitful – in the greatest way. Along the way we encounter pests that attempt to destroy us as we bud.

Faith

As we saw above, it all begins with realizing the potential we have. We have seen that we discover potential through information and revelation. Then, we must develop the capacity to harness it to achieve God's purpose and destiny.

We must walk and live by faith. Faith sees in the dark and through the dark. It is by faith that we push out or release this potential.

God told Abraham that his seed would possess the gate of his enemies (Genesis 22:17). The seed is what I refer to as potential as we saw earlier in the chapter. Also, we saw in Genesis 1, that whatever God speaks creates faith in us.

Faith is the power that sees beyond the seen to the realm of the unseen. Faith is the eyes of vision. It sees through the dark and in the dark.

As Jesus said, this faith is comparable to a mustard seed. This seed, which is small, matures into a great tree.

We have so far realized four things:

• God, the Creator has already put everything we need to fulfill our purpose in life in us.

• Our visions should never be stifled because of a lack of human support - approval, affirmation or material.

• Nothing and no one should be allowed to put our vision on hold.

• Releasing potential gives us the opportunities we need.

Creation is waiting for the manifestation of the sons of God. It is waiting for us to release our potential and take our position in God's purpose.

The road to destiny is narrow and dangerous but it is worthwhile maximizing our potential.

I dare you to go ahead and be all that God created you to be.

Don't settle for anything less!

Part III

Price

"God's kingdom is like a treasure hidden in a eld for years and then accidentally found by a trespasser. The nder is ecstatic—what a nd!—and proceeds to sell everything he owns to raise money and buy that eld.

Matthew 13:44, Message

Andrew Mutana

CHAPTER 10

THE PRICE TAG

In the month of June 2005, I got the opportunity of taking my first international flight. It was a very exciting experience. I was part of a delegation from Kenya attending an International Christian Business conference. When we landed at the Incheon airport in South Korea, we were well received and driven to a beautiful golf resort.

After the end of that conference, I was invited to go and speak at a prayer mountain in the south of the country. When I got there I was amazed at how blessed this ministry was. They seemed to own the entire hill. They had hotels, schools, a beautiful sanctuary...

One day, after ministry, I was called from my hotel. The leader of this ministry asked to take me out on a city tour. We got into her beautiful car. I enjoyed the ride which ended at one of the largest departmental stores in the city.

We parked at the six floor. As soon as we got out of the elevator we were in this apparel shop. There were all kinds of designer suits, shoes, watches and clothing. My lady host then instructed her assistant to ask me whether I wanted anything out of this store. I said no. She seemed disappointed.

Then we moved to the next floor. This place was stocked with all kinds of phones and electronics. She asked again whether I could pick whatever I needed. Again, I said no.

We moved down from store to store until we came to the lowest floor which had all kinds of groceries. At every store she would ask me to pick anything. At the last store she asked again whether there was anything she could buy for me. My answer was still no.

This time she got angry. She intructed the gentleman to just pick anything for me. When we got to the counter, she opened her purse which probably contained more than 20 cards and paid for the items.

When we got back into the car, she said this to me, "Why did you not take anything out of the store? I was ready to buy for you whatever you needed. Now you've missed this opportunity.

Did I want any of those things? Of course I did. In fact, I had been praying for most of them. God had placed someone in my life to be a blessing. She was ready to pay the price. I was not ready to receive. I guess I was foolish too.

You see, I kept looking at the price tags on the items. I learned later on that this woman was a millionare. She didn't care about the prices as much as I did. I keep hoping such an opportunity presents itself again soon. This time I may have to be stopped!

Are you willing to pay the price?

Upon entering any store every individual would help themselves to almost everything on the shelves if they were free. However, on each item is a small tag called the price tag. This separates the shoppers into two categories. There are those who are willing but are unable. There are those who are able but not willing.

Price is what divides us into social classes; where we live, what we eat and where we eat.

Every gift is treasured by its known or presumed value. There is a very interesting story in the Bible. It is one the incidents in the life of David. As you know David had a very interesting life - how he defeated Goliath, became King...

At this point, David and the entire nation of Israel were experiencing judgment from God. This was because of a mistake David had done that greatly angered God. He urgently needed to make an offering to God to stop the plague.

2 Samuel 24:24:

And the king said unto Araunah, Nay; but I will surely buy it of thee at a price: neither will I offer burnt offerings unto the Lord my God of that which doth cost me nothing. So David bought the threshing oor and the o en for fty shekels of silver.

He approached a man called Araunah. This man owned a field that David had identified as the perfect place to build an altar for God. He wanted to buy it. However, Araunah on seeing the king willingly offered it for free. David insisted that he could not offer to the Lord what cost him nothing.

The principle here is this: Whatever is worth pursuing in life has a price attached to it. You can achieve anything in life. But are you willing to pay the price?

Andrew Mutana

CHAPTER 11

THE KINGDOM PRICE

Jesus talked about the Kingdom more than any other subject. In Matthew 6:33, He said that we should seek the Kingdom first and all other things would be added to us. In Luke 11:2, He asked us to pray that His Kingdom would come.

On another occasion, Jesus shared a story of a man who discovered a field. Somewhere on this field was a pearl of great price. This man went and sold all that he had, came and bought that field (Matthew 13:44). According to this story, either this man was the only one who knew the value of this field or was the only one willing to pay the price to purchase it.

The questions are: What is this Kingdom? Where is it? How do we find it? What is the price to seek and find it?

You may be wondering now? What does the Kingdom of God have to do with the pursuit of destiny? Everything! In fact, most people use Kingdom principles every day without even realizing it. These principles work whether we are born again or not. For those who are born again, it is extremely vital to know these principles and begin to operate on them. When we do, it changes the ball game. We don't have to struggle like the rest of the people do. All that remains for us to pay the price for seeking the Kingdom – the rest falls in place.

How do you pay for something free?

Remember in the previous chapter, I shared with you my story of how I failed to pick anything in the store though my host was ready to pay. What stopped me was fear, pride, false humility and I guess some bit of foolishness.

Now when it comes to this store called 'The Kingdom of God', everything is marked free. Jesus paid for everything in full. At Calvary, He said that it was finished. Ours therefore, is really to live and walk in this finished work. Not only that. We have free access through His blood. We can walk any time, any day, ask and receive whatever we need.

It seems easy. It seems straightforward. Doesn't it?

As Peter rightly said that we are a royal priesthood. (1 Peter 2:9) We are royalty! I believe this so much that we decided to name our children Prince and Princess! I always tell the first born who is the only one not named that way that he's a king.

Now there are a few things we know about kings:

1. A King never suggests or requests. Their word is always final. They always decree what they want to happen.

2. A King has power. The Bible says in Ecclesiastes 8:4,

"Where the word of a King is there is power" As we shall see in a later

chapter, we need power to fulfill our purpose. We obtain this power when we align ourselves with the Kingdom; when we live to please our King.

The Kingdom life is the life that Heaven has already designed for us to live. It is the abundant life – living as Kings and Queens. (John 10:10)

The King is ready. Are you?

Ironically, most Christians don't live to the fullness of the purpose of God for their lives. Because of the fall, many even those in the church are not enjoying this abundant life. We often misrepresent Him and don't look like we belong to His Kingdom. We often struggle with debt, failed or dysfunctional families and many other things that unsaved people struggle with. The reason is our failure to pay the price needed to tap into the realm of God's purpose and plan for our lives.

Giving your life to Jesus is not the end. It is the genesis of the journey of the lifelong road to God's purpose and destiny for our lives. Are we willing and able to pay the price to get to the place where God wants us to be?

There is a price to pay to find and live in the kingdom – Obedience.

By grace, we can live a life of obedience and experience all that He has already done for us.

We've got to be willing and obedient to eat the best of the land. (Isaiah 1:19) His instructions are simple. His yoke is easy. The price we pay is giving up our own agendas, our goals, our will - ultimately our life.

We exchange it for His!

Nobody will do it for you! As is normally said; "If we have nothing to die for, then we haven't found something to live for." God expects you and me to play our part. - To use all that He has already put at our disposal to bring out that which he has placed in us.

CHAPTER 12

FROM BARRENNESS TO FRUITFULNESS

*I*saiah 54:1-4:

Sing, O barren, thou that didst not bear; break forth into singing, and cry aloud, thou that didst not travail with child: for more are the children of the desolate than the children of the married wife, saith the LORD.

Enlarge the place of thy tent, and let them stretch forth the curtains of thine habitations: spare not, lengthen thy cords, and strengthen thy stakes;

For thou shalt break forth on the right hand and on the left; and thy seed shall inherit the gentiles, and make the desolate cities to be inhabited.

Fear not; for thou shalt not be ashamed; neither be thou confounded; for thou shalt not be put to shame: for thou shalt forget the shame of thy youth, and shalt not remember the reproach of thy widowhood any more.

This is a prophetic word to the barren woman. In the Jewish culture, barrenness brought great shame and reproach. God spoke prophetically to the nation of Israel. He was preparing them for what He was about to do.

The children of the barren woman were going to be more than those of the married wife. But this blessing came with a price. The barren woman would have to pay the price by:

- Enlarging the place of her tent

- Stretching forth the curtains of her habitations

- Sparing not

- Lengthening her cords

- Strengthening her stakes

We will now look at this passage of scripture to see how this applies to our pursuit of destiny.

Enlarge the place of your tent

God told the barren woman to develop her capacity. Sometimes, we are so comfortable with our small place, which cannot hold the miracle that God has for us. This reminds me of the prophets who came to Elisha with a request, "The place we are in is too small". (2 Kings 6:1) Elisha challenged them to build themselves a bigger place.

Enlarging capacity may involve studying more. I guess this is what Paul had in mind as he told Timothy to study to show himself a workman that needs not be ashamed.

It could also mean praying and fasting more. It may also mean doing stuff that we don't enjoy doing; stuff that doesn't make sense today – to perform better tomorrow.

Discipline means paying the price today that we may play tomorrow. People under discipline, forfeit some comforts that other people enjoy today because they have their sight on the prize or goal in the future.

Stretch forth the curtains of your habitations

Stretching has something to do with exceeding the maximum limit of something. It means going the extra mile. Taking a decision to do more than average. Breaking out of the norm. Refusing to compromise our standards just to be accepted. Choosing excellence and shunning mediocrity.

Stretching also means that we refuse to settle in the comfort zone. We choose to launch deeper so that we can rise higher. This is the price that many are not willing to pay for their destiny. Many of us would rather swim in the familiar waters and avoid being confrontational and controversial. Yet these are two things that we cannot avoid if we choose to stretch the curtains of our habitations.

In the famous prayer of Jabez, he asked God to enlarge his coast. (1 Chronicles 4:10) You see, my friend, there is no way we will stretch our boundaries without encroaching on some other person's turf. It is a fight and a battle which we must be willing to fight; ready to settle for nothing less of total victory.

The devil is a liar. He must be forcefully evicted from all that belongs to us in Christ. The church must arise and take its rightful position.

Remember: If we are not willing to do more than we did yesterday, we limit ourselves to yesterday's results.

Spare not

This means not staying out of the areas we think are inconvenient. The Bible says of Moses that when he was mature, he chose to suffer affliction with the people of God than to enjoy the pleasures of sin for a while. (Hebrews 11:24-25)

This also reminds me of the time Saul spared the best of the sheep and oxen. He also spared Agag the king when God had asked him to destroy everything in Amalek. God dealt with him severely. (1 Samuel 15)

God requires of us to deal with whatever has to be dealt with and not to allow anything to stand in the way of our relationship with Him.

To spare not means being willing to take risk. My brother once got a message on his phone from a friend, which I found very interesting. This was the message; "It is risky not to risk".

Indeed, to get an uncommon blessing means we must also become uncommon. We must be willing to do some crazy stuff and take God at His word.

Take the limits off God! Go for it!

Lengthen thy cords

I recently heard Tommy Tenny say a very powerful statement:

"Success is when preparation meets opportunity".

God is stressing in many words that we must make room. Lengthening the cord means either buying more cord and attaching it to what we have or stretching what we have if it is elastic. Either means is costly.

One of the reason the things God wants to do in our lives delay is due to the mindset we have. As has been said, we need to change our attitude for us to change our altitude. There's no way we can defeat giants when we have a grasshopper mentality. (Numbers 13, 14).

Of the 12 spies that had been sent to spy the land, only 2 used the eyes of faith and were able to get there. These two had prepared for greatness.

The Israelites had been waiting for forty years to possess the Promised Land but ultimately they missed it because of rebellion. It is amazing how we can easily blow it all when we are so close to the fulfillment of our dreams.

Just because we cannot look at the other end of the horizon we give up at the time when our breakthrough is imminent.

We need to lengthen our cords by not limiting ourselves to our environment and circumstances. "All things are possible to those who believe," Jesus said.

Strengthen thy stakes

Nahum 2:1 says that we must fortify our power mightily. To strengthen our stakes we must dig our wells. We must consolidate our position.

It creates a picture in my mind of an army at war that has retreated to reinforce their position.

Literary, we set boundaries, which the enemy cannot cross. No matter how much pressure is applied we must not compromise.

When we read on in this chapter of Isaiah, we see that we will be able to break forth on the right and on the left. This means that nothing will be able to stop us. It also says that our seed shall inherit the Gentiles and make desolate cities to be inhabited. (Isaiah 54:3)

It's our time

As a generation, we have travailed but have not wrought much deliverance and salvation for lost humanity.

Many prophecies don't get fulfilled because we fail to prepare for them. In other words, we are not ready for them. While we are waiting for God to move, He is also waiting for us to do what He requires of us.

Anything we don't pay for is usually less valued. When we don't feel the pain of sacrificing to get something, we often easily let it slip through our hands.

Remember, we are fighting a battle against the enemy! That is why there is a price to pay in the first place. The enemy is will not let go unless we put up resistance. But as the scripture says, thanks be to God who gives us victory in Jesus Christ. (1 Corinthians 15:57)

We'll confidently say as David said, "By my God I shall overrun a troop. I shall scale a wall." (Psalm 18:29)

Chapter 13

The Price of Patience

God has designed life into seasons. Ecclesiastes 3:1 says that there is a time and season for every purpose under heaven. Life is a progression of steps or stages that cannot be skipped. There is no short-cut to success. Every season is designed to bring us to a certain degree of maturity in the pursuit of assignment.

The Word says in Ecclesiastes 8:4 that there is a time and a season for everything under the sun regardless of how heavy a burden lies on a man's heart. God makes all things beautiful in His own time. When your time has come, no one can stop you.

The hard, difficult and trying moments are those between vision and reality. We need to continually pray like David for God to show us the path of life. Or like Moses, ask Him to help us number our days so that we may apply our hearts to wisdom.

In fact, I believe that the greatest reason God allows times and seasons is to help us to develop character and obtain wisdom. As we wait patiently upon Him, He uses the process to our advantage. The price we pay in the process is never a mistake and should never be seen as such. If we develop an attitude we can get bitter in the process.

Wisdom is in discerning the seasons of life – how to be in the right places at the right time with the right information and revelation. We need discernment like the sons of Issachar. It is written that they understood the times and seasons (1 Chronicles 12:32).

Remember: Knowledge results from accumulation of facts. Wisdom only comes from revelation.

It is very important to realize that not only do we have to be patient, meaning allow time for God's purposes, we also have to appreciate that there is a season when God's purposes for our lives will be fulfilled.

By wisdom, Isaac sowed in famine and reaped a hundred fold. Wisdom like faith sees the invisible and believes the impossible. To walk in wisdom is a price more expensive than gold. Without it, we delay our progress in God's purpose.

The price of enduring criticism

The world hates dreamers. Once you are successful, people will show up to criticize you in every imaginable way. Actually, you don't even have to be successful. You just need to go out and do something – then haters will show up. It is tough when people say ugly things about us. But we can allow that criticism

to build us not break us. As is often said, "When life gives you a lemon, squeeze it and make lemonade". Get better not bitter!

Often times, people will criticize us harshly because they don't know how far we've come or the journey still ahead of us. However, as long as we ourselves understand our seasons, we should never become anxious.

Isaac was patient in the face of much opposition

In Genesis 26, Isaac faced his father's enemies who had covered his father's wells. He chose not only to uncover them but also to dig more wells.

The first wells were taken over by his enemies. This happened with the next well again and again. Each time this happened he just gave that well a name and moved on to dig another well. He refused to get distracted by the opposition. He also soldiered on despite the rejection and discouragement he got from the enemies. His persistence finally broke all his enemies' resistance and opposition.

Isaac finally had a permanent breakthrough. His enemies came to make peace with him. He called the well "Rehoboth", meaning that "the Lord has made room for us and we shall be fruitful in the land." His price had finally paid off.

Don't give up

In the same way, quitting should never be an option. Many give up when the vision lingers. Habakkuk 2:1-4 says that even when the vision lingers wait for it, for it will surely come to pass. God intentionally uses trials to work our patience. As it is written, faith works patience. It is the endurance, persistence, perseverance, long-suffering and self-control that makes a difference to this life.

James 1:2-5 says that we are to count it all joy when we face all kinds of trials. Patience works perseverance so that we become perfect wanting nothing. We must be able to hold on through the storm until we get to the other side.

In fact, failure should never be part of our vocabulary. We must decide to see failure as a temporary setback.

We should be ready to use every stumbling block as a stepping-stone to higher ground.

We should know that with God there is nothing like defeat. What seems as defeat is only a setup for our comeback and a learning experience. When beaten, we should be able to count our losses and say with courage and new determination, "Devil, I am ready to rise up again!"

Yes! A good man falls seven times and rises again. Every rising will be a leap to higher ground and greater glory.

Galatians 5:6 says that we should not be weary with well doing for in due time we shall reap if we faint not. I encourage you my friend to read this book with conviction.

Do not give up, or give in and you will win. Payday is on the way! Meditate on the principles in this book besides meditating on God's Word and let Him strengthen you!

Do not be intimidated by other people's success.

Stay secure and confident that in God's appointed time, seasons will change in your favor!

Part IV

Pain

We can ignore even pleasure. But pain insists upon being attended to. God whispers to us in our pleasures, speaks in our conscience, but shouts in our pains: it is his megaphone to rouse a deaf world.

C.S. Lewis

Andrew Mutana

CHAPTER 14

HAVE YOU CRIED YOURSELF TO SLEEP?

In the month of March 1997, I set out on a journey to look for my father. I remember very well the morning I broke the news to my mother. She was shaken. She suddenly revealed a lot of things that I didn't know about this man. I know she told me a lot of this stuff in a bid to discourage me.

"What do you really need from this him? she asked. What did I really need? I thought.

Nothing! As far as material or monetary support was concerned. By this time, I was in my second year, studying Electrical engineering at the university. We had gone through a lot. We had seen tough days. But now things were actually looking up. School tuition was no longer a problem. Life was a little bit comfortable. The government was actually giving us some money yearly to facilitate our study.

Digressing a little bit, I recall very well 4 years prior to this time, how God had helped me out right after O level. It was probably 4pm in the evening. I was dirty and sweaty after a long day working as a porter at a construction site in the small Ugandan town of Kabale.

I had heard someone call out my name. I looked up and recognized this guy as one of my former classmates. The news he broke out to me were certainly more refreshing than taking a glass of cold water on that hot day.

The national results had been released. I had emerged the best in the entire district and among the best in the country. And as if this news was not exciting enough, as soon as I got to the school, I was told that I had been awarded a scholarship for my A-level study. For the next two years everything was fully catered for.

The same scenario seemed to repeat itself after my A-levels. My results this time were not as outstanding as before. However, they were good enough to earn me a place among only 24 people countrywide who had been awarded scholarships to study Electrical Engineering at the prestigious Makerere University.

"So why don't you just focus and finish your degree? You'll be alright," she implored. "The last time I talked to your father you were only a year old. I doubt you can trace him in that big city. And even if you did, no one really knows what might happen to you. You might even get killed!" As she spoke these words, I knew she was holding back her tears. I could feel the apprehension mixed with pain probably from past memories.

But I had made up my mind. I needed closure. Besides, I was confident because I knew that God had spoken to me confirming that this was the right time. In retrospect, something greater was drawing me to Nairobi. Destiny!

In many ways my mother was right. 2 weeks later, I was holding back tears having heard words of rejection from a man I had longed to see all my life. It was so painful. I had sacrificed a lot just to get to this point.

We had finally located him. I could hear his voice as he talked to this gentleman on this old phone. "That is not my son. I don't want anything to do with him...His mother was this and this ....", he said. "Why does he hate me so much?" I wondered. He hadn't even seen me. He hadn't even talked to me. The pain was unbearable. It was probably better if he had pushed a sword right through my heart, I thought.

"That is it. I don't really need this man." I muttered with tears in my eyes. Had it not been for the lovely lady -mama John - my new found Kenyan mum scolding me, I was ready to catch the next bus and head back to Kampala.

Mama John looked at me with this no-nosense look and asked, "Did you tell me that God spoke to you?" "Yes mum", I replied. "Then don't tell me that you're pulling out of this. We will not look for him again. We'll just go back to the house and pray. He's going to look for us!" She added.

And pray we did. There is so much power in prayer. Two days later, the phone rang. I heard mama John speaking upstairs. A few minutes later, she ran down the stairs. She was elated. "Guess who is on the phone Andrew. I just talked to your Dad. He'll be on his way. You'll meet at such and such a place. We need to get ready." She spoke as she hurried up the stairs. Long story short, 2 hours later I found myself at this beautiful restuarant enjoying a meal. Sitting across the table was this man I had dreamed of knowing all my life.

But it was not what I had fantasized it would be. It was an anti-climax of sorts. A dry, emotionless conversation. In fact, it was as if we were trying to find what to talk about.

The next day, aboard a bus back to Kampala, I wondered what this had been all about. I realized that God wanted to close a chapter in my life. I had carried so much pain and bitterness for far too long. Though I **was** a child of God, the prayer leader of the University fellowship, I habored a lot of bitterness and anger towards both of my parents.

For me to get to my destiny, God wanted my heart healed. I needed to forgive my mother and my father. God began to show me that He was with me all this while. He showed me that out my pain He was going to birth a great ministry for His glory.

Now more than 20 years later, I'm thankful for everything I've been through in life. I've ministered to multitudes on the 3 continents of America, Asia and Africa. I've ministered in prisons, halfway houses, schools and streets. I've been invited to radio stations and T.V stations to share my story. Even this book you're reading right now was born out of that pain.

God gives beauty for ashes. He's made something out of a life that was broken and wounded. I've seen countless lives brought to Jesus. Most of the times, all I've had to do is share my story.

I'm not perfect. I'm still an unfinished project. But I'm determined to give God everything. At the back of my mind is always are my mother's words, "Andrew, God stopped me when I had decided to abort you. He said that when you grow up, you'll be His servant."

Give Him your pain, your broken heart and your shattered dreams. Watch what He'll do with your life!

CHAPTER 15

THE VALUE OF PAIN

It was a morning like any other. But the night had been one of the longest in my life. I hardly slept. I spent most of the time wrestling with God in prayer, in the midst of a crossroad of decision.

I was debating whether or not I should submit my resignation letter to my employer. Our first-born son had just turned one. The way I got this job was also a miracle in itself. Remember, I had been raised in much poverty. Now life was getting better. Not long before then, I had just driven my first car. Having grown up in a humble poor African background it was unheard of to own a car at 26.

That morning, I surrendered my will to His will. I rushed to the human resource office and dropped the letter at the manager's desk. I quickly rushed out as fast as my legs could carry me.

What happened after that is anyone's guess. I had to fight a series of emotions from within – fear, anxiety, insecurity ... and many battles also from without. Most of my friends thought I had lost it.

God was leading us to start a ministry in another country. We had to sell off all we had acquired and move to a place where no one knew us.

I thank God for my wife who chose to stand with me even when she couldn't understand whether or not I was making the right decision.

We went through very painful and dark moments. The journey from discovering your purpose, tapping into our potential, to reaching and walking in your destiny is very bumpy. We can never escape tests in our life's journey.

If there is one thing we must expect in this journey of life, it is pain. We also must learn (as hard as it is) that pain is valuable. Pain has no warning. It overwhelms you in a split second.

How much can we endure and still press on to the higher calling? How do we respond when people hurt us and they don't even seem to realize that they are hurting us?

Sometimes this pain is God's way of getting our attention. When we stagnate, God stirs up our nest by allowing pain. Nothing pushes us faster from the comfort zone like pain. I'm sure you've read or heard the story of Lot. He was advised by the angels to rush out of Sodom. He hesitated but eventually had to be pushed out. This is why it is better to obey God consistently than to have to compel Him to push us out of the comfort zones.

As we journey along through the seasons, pain comes in different ways and measures:

1. The pain of leaving our comfort zone:

2. The pain of being rejected and misunderstood

3. The pain of betrayal

4. The pain of failure

The pain of leaving our comfort zone

You see, my friend, when you are still going through the night season, no one wants to associate with you. People rally behind you when you've come out of the hell and the high waters as well as stormy weather.

After landing in Nairobi having resigned from my job, I remembered all of the friends back in Uganda. Most of these guys called me out often to go take a cup of coffee. I also used to help them out whenever I could. I made up a list of 50 of these friends. Then I drafted a text message - carefully detailing how I had left my job, was now in 'full-time' ministry and needed some kind of partnership. Of the 50, only 4 responded. And of the 4, only one person commited to give $3 every month!

Isn't it strange that just when you need friends most, they are out of your sight?

The pain of being rejected and misunderstood

Every time we stand out, we attract rejection. It is only human for people to criticize and disparage what we don't understand.

Joseph was rejected by his brothers. Moses faced rejection from the people God had sent him to deliver. Jesus was rejected by His own. So will you and me.

It is painful feeling being ostracized simply because of sharing a dream or vision. Yet this is one of the ways to ascertain that your vision is of great value. Every great man or woman you see had to walk alone many miles before others join him. Loneliness is painful. We all want to be accepted and supported. But as people decided to pursue our destiny, we must expect and learn how to handle such pain.

The pain of betrayal

Jesus suffered tremendous pain throughout His life. He was a man of sorrows. In my opinion, I think the greatest pain He faced was not at the cross. It was the betrayal of His friend and disciple Judas. The greatest pain we experience from people is the betrayal of friends we've trusted the most. One of the greatest examples we learn from Jesus was how He handled that betrayal.

Unfortunately, the path of life is dotted with betrayals. Absalom fought against his father and took over his concubines. Joseph was betrayed by his own brothers. Jesus was betrayed by Judas.

The best example of the betrayal faced in our day is in marriage. Imagine discovering that a spouse you've shared life together with for a long time is filing for divorce. I've heard stories of this happening without the couple having any serious arguments or crises. Questions and feelings of betrayal begin to run through the mind.

I must add at this point that as much as we need this preparation of pain, the way we handle it will determine whether we learn from our past experiences or not.

So how do we handle betrayal?

- One of the most important things is to guard against the root of bitterness (Hebrews 12:15).

- To advance to the future, you and I must learn to forgive. We should also be able to let go and release that individual(s) who have caused that pain. It is impossible to forget unless we get a memory lapse but we can smile at the memory of pain. We can remember the pain without feelings of remorse or revenge. This is purely a work of grace and can only happen by the Power of the Holy Spirit.

Hard as it is, unless we break free from the past we can never rise to a higher level.

The pain of failure

As we take a step of faith into the unknown, we make many mistakes. I've personally made many.

Failure is painful. No sane human being would wish or plan to fail. Yet as the cliché goes, "It is better to try and fail than to fail to try". Interestingly, it seems that the greatest preparation for success is failure.

So how do we use failure to our advantage?

- We should not be too hard on ourselves: We are human. Without failing it is easy to perceive that we are invincible. We are tempted to make many superficial decisions. We don't take time to include the human element of failure in our projections and calculations.

- Learn lessons of how to do it better next time: It is impossible to maintain success unless we've stood in failure.

- Use failure as the stepping stone for the next level: As long as we are flesh and blood, we will have to make mistakes and fail many times. How we respond to failure often determines whether or not we move to the next level. Wrong response causes us to stagnate or even slide back into mediocrity.

In my own life, I have encountered many terrible situations. The way I respond to them has changed as I realize that they eventually turn out for my good. I begin to see them as God's way of setting me up for another comeback.

When I look back at my life, I thank God more and more for my failures than for my successes; my valleys than for my mountains; my enemies than for my friends.

CHAPTER 16

THE PROCESS

For a period of time, I was a member of the faculty of a men's ministry here in Nairobi. My task was to teach this group of men the importance of 'Discovering our Divine Purpose.' One day having shared the same principles in this book, one of the brothers walked up to me. He summarized my session very well that day. He said to me, "Prayer sustains us in the painful process of releasing potential." One of my friends would call that a 'tweetable' quote.

Anyway, in that session I used the germination process as an illustration of the painful process of unleashing our potential. Have you ever imagined how the leaf shoot breaks through the hard soil of the ground?

Ironically, life comes out of a dead thing. When a seed is planted, that is just the beginning. The water and the warmth in the ground help to soften its hard surface. It then has to die. That process means that the seed will lose its original identity.

Then the plumule slowly breaks out of the soil into the unknown world where it now faces the vagaries of weather and the scorching sun.

What keeps it going for a while is the reservoir stored in the cotyledons. It is not surprising therefore that not all seeds blossom and germinate well. Some die, others wither, while others don't even break out of the ground. This plant will need constant care and watering.

Metaphorically, I believe that as far as our lives are concerned, prayer is the water that is needed at every stage of development of this crop called Potential.

The first stem that anchors this plant, subsequently holding the branches and the fruit is what I categorise as passion.

Suffice to say, producing fruit is a process - A process, which is tough and selective. The branches have to put up with the wind and heat. When the buds appear, they die too and give way for the flowers. The flowers will also wither with time giving way to the fruit.

Using this analogy, it is certain that by the time we arrive at our destiny – walking in God's purpose for our lives, we have been through a rigorous and painful process.

Clearly, not many people want to take this path. Most people would rather settle for a mundane, less painful, predictable and secure life. Sadly, by so doing, they rob themselves of the joy and fulfillment of a life lived fully.

Pursuit of destiny is very painful. This is why life is full of starters but very few finishers. Will we endure to the end for the fruit?

Being pruned for more fruit

Interestingly, Jesus used a similar analogy while emphasizing the need for His disciples to stay connected to Him.

John 15:1-2:

I am the true vine, and my Father is the husbandman.

Every branch in me that beareth not fruit He taketh away: and every branch that beareth fruit, He purgeth it, that it may bring forth more fruit.

Jesus talked about the relationship between the branches and the vine. He showed that without remaining connected to the vine, no branch can produce fruit. The interesting reality though is that when a branch does produce fruit, it is subjected to more pruning.

Similarly, the process works ultimately for our good.

1. It is carefully designed by God himself to shape us to handle what He has prepared for us. This is why it is very disastrous to short circuit the process. We end up half-baked and whatever is placed in our hands just passes through. I'm sure you've heard the saying, "The blessing in the hand of a fool is a curse."

2. Just as fire is used to take away the dross from the silver, pain and affliction refine us. For gold to be purified, it has to be passed through a very hot furnace of fire. Actually, practically, all the most precious earthly things require intense preparation.

3. God has used pain in my life many times to harden my resolve.

4. Many times the things I went through revealed hidden or latent potential within me. And at other times, I obtained clarity and direction in those hard times.

5. Glory comes out of broken vessels. The greater the pain, the greater the glory. The anointing, which literary means oil, only comes out of fruits or seeds that have been squeezed. It is this squeezing process that we all wouldn't want to go through. It is a death process that causes the seed to resurrect and bear much fruit. Once crushed the anointing flows.

6. Great athletes have to endure extreme mental and physical training to make it to the top. The process is not just about getting to that place – when you have realized your purpose and are walking in it. It is about being able to sustain yourself there – gaining stability and finishing strong. We all know that staying at the top is much harder than getting there. Such athletes inculcate in them a discipline to keep fit. This discipline is very painful to the body since our bodies hate it.

7. Lastly, we should appreciate the process as the avenue, which God will use to increase our faith. When things seem to be going from bad to worse, we know that the testimony of our deliverance will also be glorious.

In Romans, Paul wrote that he considered the momentary afflictions as not worthy to be compared to the glory that will be revealed.

Your mess is your message. You can only give people what you have!

And you can only take people where you have been.

CHAPTER 17

HOW PAIN HELPS YOUR PURPOSE

Enveloped within adversity is opportunity. We must welcome it with an attitude of using it to our advantage. Pain is always a springboard or launching pad to greater success and fulfillment. Every stumbling stone becomes a stepping-stone to higher ground.

1. Pain gives our prayers fervency and a depth

We praise God without reservation knowing where He got us. Even our worship is fervent and real because like Paul we see our lives being poured out as a drink offering. Jabez was born in sorrow. The pain he experienced had caused him to pray a radical prayer. This famous prayer moved him into a sphere of influence. From obscurity he became a great leader.

2. Pain pushes out your potential

Every human being is born with a desire to prove to the world who they are. All children have grand dreams of what they will become when they grow up. This desire is God given. Sadly, not many people live to achieve their childhood dreams. Many fall off along the way. Others resign to what they call their fate. They simply follow the path of least resistance. The reason a few stand out is because of resilience. Resilient people have a resolve that they'll bounce back no matter what happens. This resolve is even made stronger when people dismiss them. My potential has lit brightest in the darkest moments. Often my enemies pushed me to the direction of my destiny. This is because they said things about me or did terrible things to me that all enhanced my determination to make it.

3.   Pain stirs up faith

Till we hit the bottom, we will not find the necessity to seek God in a deeper way. It is a prayer that we pray when we are near desperate and all our hope is in God that will cause miracles to happen. At such uncertain times we have reached what is called the zero hour or the end of the rope.

The children of Israel cried out to God by reason of their taskmasters (Exodus 1). The pain of bondage was so great that they yearned for freedom. God listened to their cry. He sent Moses to deliver them with mighty signs.

4.   Pain balances our lives

Life has to be balanced by pain. Just as we cannot have mountains without valleys, and no roads without bends and bumps, without challenge, we cannot avoid becoming proud and boastful. We may be tempted to think that we have made it on our own. God's ways are beyond comprehension. He will always use the most unexpected and unqualified vessels. As Paul says in I Corinthians 1:29, God will use the weak things to confound the strong, the despised things and the things that are not. That no flesh will glory in His presence!

5.   Pain prepares us to minister to others

The best preparation for ministry comes from pain. Every truly anointed man or woman of God has been through something. Without pain or sacrifice, it is very hard to develop a servant spirit, which is very crucial in this day and age.

6.   Pain teaches us patience

James 1:2-4:

My brethren, count it all joy when ye fall into divers temptations;

Knowing this that the trying of your faith worketh patience.

But let patience have her perfect work that you may be perfect and entire, wanting nothing.

Isn't it amazing that James is telling his readers to count it all joy when they face all kinds of trials? That is a rare sermon in our days. We all want to pray and work ourselves out of every kind of trial. The last thing we ever want to do is rejoice! Yet according to this text, we need patience to become perfect.

Blessed but limping

As we complete this chapter, what better way to summarize than to look at the story of Jacob. In the book of Genesis 32:22-32, we read a very interesting story of Jacob's encounter with God. Jacob was tired of his name and his life. His name meant thief, supplanter and grabber. He had hustled his way through life. Now he was getting ready to face his older brother whose birthright he had mischievously swindled with the help of his mother.

He needed God's help. He knew that without divine intervention he was faced with possibly even death. So what does he do? He sends all his family, servants and possessions ahead of him and remains alone. While alone, he has this amazing encounter of wrestling with God. He was determined to get his blessing that even when God asked him to let go, he refused.

Eventually, God blessed him, changed his name and released him from whatever was hindering his destiny as a prince with God.

Jacob's encounter and wrestling with God left him limping. Though blessed, he endured a limp throughout his life. This disability left him always conscious of where his help and strength came from.

It seems like God will allow situations in our lives to remind us that it is His grace that is at work in our lives. It is not by our strength or ability. When we falter and fail, we develop a dependency on divine help knowing full well that without Him we can do nothing. (John 15:4)

It is by the stripes of Jesus that we are healed. In the same way, oftentimes God will allow stripes on us for another's healing.

Paul once spoke of a thorn in his flesh. He cried to the Lord three times to remove it. God's reply was that His grace was sufficient. He told him that His strength is made perfect in weakness.

Paul then said that he rejoiced in weakness, tribulations and adversity. For when he is weak then he will be strong. We should likewise rejoice in God knowing that He is sovereign.

Painful as it may be, we ought to thank Him for the thorn in the flesh. Without the thorn, we would never realize that His grace is sufficient. He has designed everything – including our pain to work towards His purpose.

Andrew Mutana

CHAPTER 18

BEFORE THE PRIZE THERE IS A CROSS

Hebrews 5:7,8

Who in the days of His esh, when He had offered up prayers and supplications with strong crying and tears unto Him that was able to save Him from death, and was heard in that He feared;

Though He were a Son, yet learned He obedience by the things which He suffered;

This scripture shows us how Jesus endured pain and learned obedience by the things He suffered. True worship is obedience to the Lordship of the Master. Total and absolute surrender that says, "Thy will be done and not mine". (Matthew 6:10) This can only come through suffering. For the body to obey fully, it has to be subjected to a process of self-denial. Of course the church today has shunned such a teaching.

No wonder there is no glory in the church as yielded and obedient vessels are scarce. We are all concerned with giving our bodies the best comfort we can afford. But Jesus himself said that whoever comes after Him must be ready to carry his cross, deny himself and follow Him.

Pain, adversity, affliction or whatever one may call it, always acts as a midwife.

1. It helps us to press in to our destiny.

2. As long as we are called according to His purpose, even the worst of circumstances turn out for our good (Isaiah 3:10), (Romans 8:28).

Paul in Philippians 3:13, 14 gives us a formula.

Brethren, I count not myself to have apprehended: but this one thing I do, forgetting those things that are behind, and reaching forth unto those things which are before,

I press toward the mark for the high calling of God in Christ Jesus.

What does Hebrews 12:2 tell us about Jesus?

Looking unto Jesus the author and   nisher of our faith; who for the joy that was set before Him endured the cross, despising the shame, and is set down at the right hand of the throne of God.

The greater the affliction; the greater the glory.

Jesus endured the cross and scorned its shame because His eyes were on the glory.

Remember: In Psalms 126, the Word says this; *he that goes forth weeping bearing precious seed shall doubtless come back rejoicing, bringing the sheaves with him.*

Draw the line in the sand, count your losses, forget the past and press on to the future.

Andrew Mutana

Part V

Passion

Light yourself on re with passion and people will come from miles to watch you burn.

John Wesley

Andrew Mutana

CHAPTER 19

How Bad Do You Want It?

$G_{alatians\ 6:9:}$

And let us not be weary in well doing: for in due season we shall reap, if we faint not.

A few years ago, the world was amazed by the determination of one Kenyan called Hyvon Ngetich. This lady who had participated in the Austin, Texas marathon refused to quit the race when her legs could not carry her any longer. The 29-year-old spent the final 50 yards on her hands and knees until she crossed the finish line.

She refused to lose. She still managed to come in third. But contrary to expectation, because of her perseverance and determination, the race officials gave her the money for second place – the position she would have attained if she hadn't fallen.

To me, passion is simply strong desire; a desire that is irresistible. When one has passion, they refuse to be denied. They don't settle for second place. They will always aim for the top, excellence and the prize.

I believe passion is also synonymous or a combination of enthusiasm, zeal, resilience, tenacity and determination.

When a marriage loses passion it dies. It goes through a divorce or a separation. Marriages can withstand a lot of stuff when there is passion. It really doesn't matter what they go through. Sometimes, they face financial struggles, other times infidelity. As long as the passion is there, they will survive the worst of situations. When that centre cannot hold anymore, they fall apart.

Conversely, when an individual loses passion, he dies. They may still go on with life. They may still report for work, raise kids and go through all the motions. But they are impotent.

Hannah and Peninah

One of the stories that inspires me most is the story of Hannah in the book of 1Samuel 1. She was most loved by her husband but was barren. The other woman in her life (Peninah) had children. She always provoked her every time they went to sacrifice to the Lord. One day Hannah felt she had had enough. She prayed a very radical prayer that the high priest Eli thought she was drunk.

You see, the greatest blessing here for Hannah came through her archrival Peninah. I didn't realize this myself till later in life. Her provocation pushed Hannah to the limit.

God answered her prayer. She gave birth to a male child. I can hear Hannah in my spirit, quietly thanking Peninah for making life unbearable for her.

In the natural, for a delivery to take place, there must be midwives. Some of the midwives are very rough. They know that any carelessness would put the life of the child and the mother at a great risk. So, they encourage the women to push.

The fight of our lives

Ephesians 6:12-13:

For we wrestle not against esh and blood, but against principalities, against powers, against the rulers of darkness of this world, against spiritual wickedness in high places.

Wherefore take unto you the whole armour of God, that ye may be able to withstand in the evil day, and having done all, to stand.

Many soldiers fight and win in the war but are carried away wounded. Others die later due to battle fatigue. Still others cannot celebrate the victory because they are carried away as prisoners of war.

The spiritual battle is even more complex because we are fighting with a very organized enemy who is unseen.

Verse 13 above talks about two things – withstanding and standing. It is possible to withstand in the evil day yet fail to stand.

The enemy knows this and he keeps throwing things to us in life to weary us. We fight through them. Though we overcome, oftentimes our passion has been lost. We have developed an attitude or have become bitter. We have withstood and survived but we cannot stand.

To stand, the Word says, we must be constantly alert and with our weapons of war in place. Satan's goal is to frustrate the purposes of God. He doesn't have to kill a people with vision if he can distract them. Remember: It is possible to be sidetracked yet doing the right thing. It is a great discipline to remain focused. To keep on the path, to keep our vision clear and remain consistent should be our focus in life.

We all go through times when what we are doing doesn't make sense. Life's fatal blows don't respect our education or lack of it, our poverty or riches, our background, beauty or status. Everybody at some point faces a battle. How we respond is very critical to our survival first and later to our thriving. God said that we shall go through the fire and water (Isaiah 43) but we will not be harmed. He promised to be with us.

Until the fruit is seen, the budding process is normally very frustrating. People don't stand with us in the budding stage; they normally rally behind us when they see success. The biggest fight therefore, is to hold on until we are where God wants us to be.

Storms are inevitable

I remember when hurricane Katrina landed at the Gulf coast of the U.S.A. The city of New Orleans was the worst hit. People woke up one morning and were overwhelmed that overnight all their life savings had been wiped away; their dreams and aspirations all had vanished; their homes and property had been swept by the floodwaters. People had to start from scratch. It is such times that really test human resilience.

Obviously, other survivors just threw in the towel inspite of all the goodwill that the world had presented to them. These might have been overwhelmed by a sense of hopelessness. And where there is no hope, there is no faith. Because faith is the substance of things hoped for.

No one chooses their disappointments, failures and struggles. Most of the time they come unexpectedly. Only those who resist the enemy will rise to use the opportunity in the calamity to move even to higher ground.

Do you feel trapped?

Let's see Ecclesiastes 9:12:

For man also knoweth not his time: as the shes that are taken in an evil net, and as the birds that are caught in the snare; so are the sons of men snared in an evil time, when it falleth suddenly on them.

We are told here that we are all ensnared in evil times as a bird gets caught in a trap.

Everything in this world that we lean on is going to be shaken one day. Only that which is unshakeable shall stand. Jesus talked about two builders. One built his house on sand and the other on a rock. They both faced a storm, winds and terrible situations. While one survived, the other one totally collapsed.

We need the foundation of His Word to withstand stormy weather. After the pain, tears, fears, evil feelings of betrayal and rejection, we should stand.

The true test of the authenticity of faith is in the fire. Peter says that faith, which is more precious than gold must go through fire.

It is easier to keep passion in good times. But what do we do when all hell breaks loose? What do we do when we can see no way?

As the famous song says, "What do you when you've given your all and it seems like it is never enough? You just stand!"

We must be able to carry ourselves off the ground when we fall. The righteous man falls seven times and rises up again.

He just counts his losses, shakes off the dust and marches on to success. As is said, "Success is failure turned inside out." It is always darkest before dawn.

Chapter 20

Passion and Your Dream

How do you and I keep our dreams alive and not let them die? A dream, like an unborn baby, can be aborted, miscarried, or stillborn.

Recently I asked a group of people to give me reasons why any pregnant woman would make a choice to abort her unborn baby.

Here are some of the answers I received:

- Fear

- Shame

- Financial limitations or bondage

- Lack of willingness to take up responsibility

- Rejection or abandonment

- Wrong timing

- Peer pressure

- Lack of support from mentors, parents...

- Selfishness
- Lack of proper knowledge of who they are – struggle with identity

This is certainly not an exhaustive list. However, as we went through this list, we realised that one thread – a lack of passion to keep the baby alive.

You see, interestingly, even with all these challenges or even worse ones existing, there are mothers who still chose to keep their babies. Their love for the baby exceeded the fear of the unknown.

Without trivializing such a weighty matter, allow me to submit to you that people fail to pursue their destiny because of precisely the same reasons.

Passion is very vital to your dream

Passion is what helped Joseph go through the pit and prison and still make it to the palace.

How could he gather the courage to face his enemies (his biological brothers) who threw him in the pit? It was still because of his passion. His dream was bigger than his problems - even himself. He recognised that God has placed him in his position to help many others.

How could he not have an attitude, be prejudiced or harbour bitterness and revenge in the face of betrayal and neglect from people who should have done better? Passion.

The link between prayer, pain and passion

Power follows passion. Where there is no passion, there is no power.

God says that the prayer, which accomplishes much, has to be fervent (James 4:16). This is another word for boiling point. The power it releases is so great because it is full of passion.

Without pain, it is hard to even talk about passion. Real passion is response to the painful things that we sense either physically or spiritually. Moreover, pain ignites lost passion. When we think of the things we have survived, our faith is stirred up to believe God for greater things. No one can ever be greater than his/her experience. It has been said that invention is a result of necessity. When we are under intense pressure, some things of intrinsic value begin to come out of our lives.

Intense pain only reveals that potential is on its way out. Nothing is worth living for that we cannot die for.

There is a place we can get to when the passion for our dream transcends what we are going through. That is when we are grateful to God for everything we've been through. Joseph had this attitude. He told his brothers that it was the Lord's doing and he had been sent before them to preserve posterity in the earth.

Passion killers

Two passion killers are fatigue and discouragement. A heart that is wearied down becomes apathetic and complacent. It lacks the drive to get to the next level. It simply settles for business as usual.

Luke 21:34:

And take heed to yourselves, lest at any time your hearts be overcharged with surfeiting, and drunkenness, and the cares of this life, and so that day come upon you unawares.

Jesus warned that we should not allow our hearts to be weighed down by drunkenness and the cares of this life lest His coming take us by surprise. It is possible to get so drunk with the fight of life and lose the sobriety needed to make sound decisions.

We need to be sober to keep moving in the direction of our dreams with clarity. To avoid fatigue and stress, we should be sensitive to the level of activity we allow ourselves to get ensnared. We should avoid fighting battles knowing that the battle belongs to the Lord. We should be able to say NO to lesser priorities. We need to rest and reserve energy for major battles.

What we are supposed to do is what we are built for. When we don't set boundaries and know our limitations, we die before our time.

We fail to be effective in the area in which we have been called, having spent all our energy trying to accomplish another man's assignment.

Even under the anointing, we still have our limitations because we carry this treasure in earthen vessel.

CHAPTER 21

THE PASSION OF JESUS

*H*ebrews 12:1-3:

Wherefore seeing we also are compassed about with so great a cloud of witnesses, let us lay aside every weight, and the sin which doth easily beset us, and let us run with patience the race that is set before us,

Looking unto Jesus the author and the   nisher of our faith; who for the joy that was set before Him endured the cross, despising the shame, and is set down at the right hand of the throne of God.

For consider Him that endured such contradiction from sinners against himself, lest ye be wearied and faint in your minds.

Often times, the word passion is used when referring to love. I watched the movie 'Passion of the Christ' by Mel Gibson. It was unfathomable how Jesus endured such pain. Some of the scenes were very hard to bear. They seemed too graphic. Yet much as this was the best description of what could have happened at Calvary, it still falls short of biblical accounts. It was a grisly and ruthless experience.

We see three things from this text about the passion of Jesus that we can learn from:

1.   Passion kept Jesus on the cross when He had the power to get off (Acts 1:3)

It is this passion to see lost humanity saved that kept Jesus on the cross. Though He was God, He was also 100% human and felt all the pain as any human would. He heard all the insults hurled at Him and could have been tempted to answer back but He did not revile. He felt that deep pain of being betrayed by a friend (Psalms 22:12-18, Psalms 41:9).

2.   His passion was more than just a desire or wish

Jesus' passion actually consumed Him. After He drove out the moneychangers and traders from the temple, He quoted a scripture from the Old Testament. This scripture says, "The zeal of thine house has consumed me".

3.   His passion helped him persevere in very tough circumstances

His passion enabled Him to endure the cross and scorn its shame. He paid the ultimate price for the salvation of humanity. Whereas none of us will ever have such a calling, we also need such passion when faced with the temptation to give up. Jesus refused to give up. He emerged out of hell and the grave a victor. He conquered all. He never became a victim of his predicament. He is the ultimate example of how we can live a victorious Kingdom life.

Paul says in 2 Corinthians 5:14, that the love of Christ constrains us. We have His perfect example. If He overcame, then we too can overcome. We need a baptism of His passion. Without passion, it is impossible to accomplish anything.

The first love

God wants passion for Him back in His church. This is why He rebuked the church in Revelation 2 that they had lost their first love. Yes, they had resisted wrong doctrines but in their struggle they had failed to maintain passion.

We all must come to the place of our first love. Jesus cried out, "The zeal of my house has consumed me".

May God revive us and light the fire again.

Andrew Mutana

CHAPTER 22

WORLD CHANGERS

The life of Samson is one of the most intriguing in the Bible. One day, while reading about his affair with Delilah, I realized one thing. Samson was so indulged by her enticement that he overlooked the enemy's strategy of ensnaring him. He disclosed the secret of his strength as a result of which he was stripped of his strength and had to wait for his hair to grow again before he could avenge his enemies. While meditating on this story, I was impressed with a revelation that Samson was unlike any ordinary man. God's anointing in his life made a difference.

The anointing of God actually sets ordinary people apart thus making them different. They do extra-ordinary things. Everybody has God given potential. However, only a few live to realize this potential. Few enjoy the benefits of maximized potential. Even fewer know what it is to live a fulfilled life.

Why is this so? It is because many individuals get trapped in comfort zones. They settle for a mediocre life – to which they don't belong. They eat dust with chicken when they ought to fly with eagles. They choose to live ordinarily. They get a job, raise a family and pursue a career like everybody else.

All these are good things to do. However, people who change the world live for more than these. Such people do more than ordinary. They reach out to the divine potential inside of them and make things happen that change the course of history. They dare to be history makers and mountain movers. They are not part of the problem but part of the solution. They are determined to make their lives count.

The passion in them is insatiable. They go for goals that everybody has given up on. They see the invisible and therefore do the impossible. Even when they go through the valley of Baca they make it a well of springs (Psalms 84:6-7). The valley of Baca is meant to be a place of sorrow and pain. But their heart is set on pilgrimage. So, they cause it to be a place of blessing. The Bible says that they go from strength to strength.

This brings us to the point where we study how we can keep our passion burning. Let's see the scripture below in Proverbs.

Proverbs 4:20-27:

My son, attend to my words; incline thine ear unto my sayings.

Let them not depart from thine eyes; keep them in the midst of thine heart.

For they are life unto those that nd them, and health to all their esh.

Keep thy heart with all diligence; for out of it are the issues of life.

Put away from thee a froward mouth, and perverse lips put far from thee.

Let thine eyes look right on, and let thine eyelids look straight before thee.

Ponder the path of thy feet, and let all thy ways be established.

Turn not to the right hand nor to the left: remove thy foot from evil.

From this text we can extract several things that we need to do as world changers.

Set our hearts on pilgrimage

While studying stability in a physics class, we were taught that there are three levels of stability: unstable, stable and intermediate. For something to be stable, it has to endure the shaking and get back to its point of equilibrium.

In verses 25-27 of Proverbs 4 above, we are told that our eyes should look right on. When we stay focused, no external pressure can push us off our path to destiny and victory. As we read earlier in Psalms 84, those who stay focused move from strength to strength.

Paul put it this way, "one thing I do is to forget what is behind and press on to the mark of the high calling in Christ Jesus" (Philippians 3:14). Forgetting what is behind means forgetting both successes and failures – everything that is past whether good or bad.

Many times it is the good things that stop us from getting the better. Mediocrity stops us from attaining excellence. Settling for the norm stops us from realizing the fullness of the potential within us. We should refuse to get our eyes off the prize!

Keep our face before God

David says in Psalm 16:8, 11,

I have set the LORD always before me: because he is at my right hand, I shall not be moved.

Thou wilt shew me the path of life: in thy presence is fullness of joy; at thy right hand there are pleasures for evermore.

There are two powerful principles that David employed in his life. First, he recognized the source of potential and the master of his destiny. It is God who shows us the path of life. Any man-made dream can fail. But whatever is born of God overcomes the world. We, therefore, must stay in His presence that He may guide us day by day into His will for our lives.

Secondly, he knew that as long as he stayed in the presence of God, he would never be moved. In Isaiah 40:31, we are reminded that even young men get exhausted and the youth give up. As a child of God, you have a resource that can never dry up. Strength has a limit. So does money, power, connections, beauty and all the great things of this world. But prayer is our means of tapping into the realm of the supernatural that is unsearchable and unlimited. Only prayer can regenerate lost passion. We will be able to run and not grow weary; walk and not faint.

Keep our hearts with all diligence

The soul is the seat of our emotions, intellect and will. It is often referred to rightly as the heart. Dreams, ideas and imaginations spring from the heart. This is where the creative power of the seed also comes from. Satan's target in his attacks on our lives is our hearts. His (satan's) desire is to get our hearts bitter, wounded, insensitive and wearied down. If we are to maintain our zeal and passion then we must guard our hearts above everything else.

As we experience tough times, our focus should be keeping our hearts from getting wounded. Wounds attract flies. In the same way, wounded hearts will always attract wrong relationships, ungodly alliances and habits. All these lead to a flawed character. If they do get wounded then we should first run to God's presence and find healing and restoration there. After pouring our hearts to God, we can then run to our pastor, a trusted confidant, a psychiatrist or a counsellor.

Running to men often gives us anesthesia for our pain when what we need is healing.

Without healing of the broken heart, tranquilizers or anti-depressants will not help. It is like treating an infection with just a pain killer. We really have to take off the masks and confront the real issues. If we don't, we'll easily end up hooked on wrong stuff – drugs, porn… as we try to medicate the pain.

David is a clear example of a man who knew the source of his

restoration. In Psalm 23:3, he speaks of how God restored his soul. He knew how to retreat. He would allow God to lead him beside still waters. There he would be refreshed.

One other way of being restored is worship. When we worship God, we drink from the river that flows from His presence. This river flushes the junk out of our spirits (Psalm 46:4).

Watch our lips

When we are under attack we are most likely to say things that ensnare us. We should pray that God helps us to keep a watch on our lips (Psalm 141:3).

In such times, we need to allow God to fight for us(Exodus 14:14). It is time to wait for divine attestation other than trying to give people a piece-of-our-mind.

When we stand still, we hasten our deliverance. Our critics soon realize that they are fighting a lone battle and chill. This does not mean that all criticism is bad nor does it mean that we should allow ourselves to be trampled on.

I'm simply saying that we should give a place to God to show that He is our salvation. As He says in Isaiah 54:17, every tongue that is raised against us in judgment, He will condemn.

We overcome more battles with our mouths shut than when open.

Nehemiah is a perfect example of a leader who faced intense opposition. He refused to respond to his enemies in the same way they came at him. He succeeded in finishing the wall within 52 days!

He was mocked by his enemies. Imagine being told that even a fox can cause the wall you are building to collapse!

He chose to keep drawing his strength from God. Not even once was his passion affected.

The enemy's plan is to zap our energy by causing us to open our mouth when we shouldn't. He then uses our words against us to ignite a fire we cannot extinguish.

But we can rest assured that when we stand for the truth we always succeed.

For the truth outlives a lie.

Andrew Mutana

Part VI

Provision

Prosperity is simply having enough of God's provision to complete his assignment in your life.

Mike Murdock

Andrew Mutana

CHAPTER 23

TAPPING INTO DIVINE PROVISION

Nora Lam was a great Chinese missionary whom God used greatly around the world. Her story was also the main inspiration behind the movie China Cry. I was blessed to hear one of the testimonies of God's provision for one of her crusades in Taiwan. This was shared by a friend who had the opportunity of meeting Nora and hearing it firsthand.

One day, as she prayed after moving to the US, God spoke to her to go to Taiwan and hold a large crusade. She did not have the money. But having been raised under Kathryn Kulmann, she believed in doing it big – for the glory of God. So she took a flight to Taiwan and asked around for the biggest venue.

This turned out to be a massive stadium normally used for major sports activities. She inquired how much it would cost to hold a meeting at this venue. It was such a huge amount that she knew only God could provide her with such resources. She would also need to do a lot of publicity campaigns to get people to come and fill that stadium.

She just started praying around this stadium. After some time, she boldly asked for permission to see the management. Once she got in, she was asked who she was and she introduced herself this way; "My father owns cattle on a thousand hills." On hearing this, the manager was so excited and exclaimed, "Wow! So you're the daughter of a very wealthy rancher!

Then, he immediately ordered that the stadium be booked for her that weekend. Interestingly, there was a very important sports fixture due to take place that time. But this manager was too impressed and had it moved to a different time. This manager also offered to help Nora with advertising – indicating to her that all the costs would be lumped together.

And these guys – the stadium management used a substantial amount of money. Soon she was on all major radio and T.V networks.

When the day came for the meetings, the stadium was fully parked. Up to this moment, she had no idea where the money would come from. At the end of every service, they would take an offering. Amazingly, on the last day when she received the report, the money given as offering was more than enough to pay the stadium management for all costs.

Within every vision is enough power for its sustenance

There is always provision for every God ordained vision. This provision only comes as we pursue the purpose. God appoints men in our path that He will use to partner with what He has called us to do. Such men will not respond to our needs. But they will respond to the vision.

I like the words of this great missionary to China:

God's work done in God's way will never lack God's supply (Hudson Taylor)

The difficulty comes in the fact that there are different levels depending on the stage of growth or fruition. I'll give these levels here as: Not enough, enough and more than enough. I'll expound on them in the next chapter.

Releasing divine provision

Furthermore, I have learned that the secret to releasing divine provision is threefold:

1-   Creating an atmosphere for God to speak.

2-   Grabbing-a-hold of the revelation.

3-   Walking in the revelation.

Creating the atmosphere

We talked about creating an atmosphere earlier on as we talked about releasing potential. The principle is the same here. Instead of focusing on the lack, we have to allow God to brood over our situation and speak a creative word that will unlock the provision we need.

2 Kings 4 speaks of a widow who was in debt and needed a miracle. When she spoke to Elisha, Elisha gave her an instruction. All she needed was to act on the word of the man of God. She was told to borrow vessels and fill them with oil. Her obedience caused her to break into a realm of unlimited, unhindered supply.

Grabbing-a-hold of the revelation

It all begins with the spiritual realm, which is unseen. Once we hear that Word, we need to grab it. Then, the light is turned on and we receive a revelation. That revelation creates faith and triggers miracles.

Walking in the revelation

Walking in the revelation is walking by faith. You don't wait until all the pieces are together! An amazing truth is seen in Genesis 1. On the first day, God spoke light to come forth. However, it was not until the fourth day that He created the objects to provide the light. This means that for three days there was light in the absence of the sun, moon and stars.

Likewise, often our situation does not match with our revelation. For example, many times when we sow our seed, we expect to reap the next day. This doesn't happen just as it wouldn't in the natural.

However, as we keep on pressing on, we will reap in due season if we faint not (Galatians 6:9).

In other words, to walk in the divine provision, we must move from the natural means and sources and tap into the supernatural means. When Jesus had to feed the 5000 families, He used a small boys lunch. His faith brought forth the multiplication.

We serve Jehovah Jireh who is our provider. He always knows our needs beforehand. (Matthew 6:8) Some miracles are instant, others take time.

If He said it, He is God enough to fulfil it. Never mind if it seems impossible in the natural.

Andrew Matana

Chapter 24

Stages/Seasons of Provision

One Sunday morning, my pastor talked about the stages of birth. Immediately, the Holy Spirit quickened me to understand a very important truth – how to tap provision for purpose.

When a mother conceives a child within her womb, everything the child will need for survival is provided for in the womb. The child is connected to the mother through the umbilical cord. Through this channel, it receives all the nutrients it needs for the 9 months of the gestation period.

This is a stage where the baby is restricted to its support system. Sadly, many of us walk through life the same way. We're hooked to our jobs and pay checks. The system of the world teaches us to look at our employer as our source, thereby limiting our vision to whatever we have been offered instead of trusting God for greater rewards.

As an example, while in Egypt, the Israelites lived in oppression under their taskmasters. They worked so hard but all their taskmasters did was give them something small – enough to maintain them so they would come to work the next day.

I personally believe that we are not supposed to spend our prime years studying and the rest of the years paying up loans and mortgages. God created us to be driven by purpose and not just doing a job because we have to. Most of us live on credit hence living in the future without enough resources for the present. We end up driving cars and living in homes that really don't belong to us. Our legacy to our children is fast becoming credit card debt, liabilities and court cases. This is a system designed by hell itself to keep us in a cycle of poverty.

Remember: Your job can never finance your God ordained vision.

It is very hard to break away from this mindset because it guarantees security and an income. However enticing it may be, as a child of God you must break away from it (the pay-check mentality) to walk in divine prosperity. This does not mean that you should leave your job. Rather, you should see it as just one stream of God's provision. Why leave your life to fate when you can allow God to change and control your destiny?

God and His Word – that's all you need!

As we saw in Genesis 1:1, when God started the work of creation, He spoke things into existence. His Word was the power to create. He called things that were not to be. (Romans 4:17)

When I preach this, I occasionally point out that every product label has a list of the ingredients used in its making. God's label had 'nothing' on it!

Jentezen Franklin said, "When you get down to nothing, God is up to something."

Jesus came that we may walk in the blessing of Abraham. Our lives can only prosper as our souls (minds) prosper (3 John 2). The truth is that God does not want us to be in debt. He wants us to have enough to fulfil His purpose for our lives. And as the truth transforms us, we will experience His abundance.

As is written in 2 Corinthians 9:6-8, *God is able to make all grace abound to us that we have all su   ciency in all things and are able to do good when there is need.*

Just enough

Purpose is never a destination. It is a journey. And this journey to our destiny is a journey of faith. God keeps revealing and unlocking new potential out of our lives as we seek Him and His leading. Every potential coming out of us demands a new level of responsibility and provision. As our faith grows, God can entrust us with the wealth of the earth to support the expanded vision.

The wilderness season is the season of just enough. It is a season of humbling and testing when we only have enough for each day. In this season God weans us from every support system. The children of Israel had a similar experience. They were commanded not to hoard supplies for the next day. Those who insisted on doing so found maggots in their food.

God was teaching them a lesson of trusting Him every day and walking by faith. The scriptures say that the just shall by faith. Without faith it is impossible to please God. (Hebrews 11:6)

The Israelites spent 40 years in the wilderness. All this time God was still getting Egypt out of them. They received manna and meat every single day. Having enough food and clothing was not their concern. God made sure their needs were met but it was always just enough for the day. (Matthew 6:8)

Can you imagine eating the same menu for 40 years? No wonder, they started missing the cucumber, garlic and onions in Egypt! They complained and murmured. They preferred a life of bondage to a life of learning to trust in God and walking the faith walk.

God says that through this season, He was teaching them that man does not live by bread alone but by every word that comes from the mouth of God (Deuteronomy 6:3,4, Matthew 4:4). In other words, this season was preparing them for the next season. God was taking them to a land flowing with milk and honey. He wanted them to learn to put their trust and confidence in Him. He alone was to be their source of supply.

More than enough

After the plagues and the Passover, the Israelites left Egypt. The Bible says that they plundered it. They were transformed from poor slaves to very wealthy people overnight. It was a classic rags-to-riches story. They took all the gold and precious metals in Egypt. In the wilderness they could not do any commerce. This is what I see as more than enough. God, while supplying their daily needs ensured that they had enough wealth to pass on to more than one generation.

Are you ready to handle more than enough?

As we pursue destiny, we all have to go through these seasons. Most people stop at the inadequacy stage. They are afraid all their lives to leave 'Egypt'. They settle for a mediocre, limited life and never get to fulfill their purpose, mission and destiny that God planned for them. Even as we pursue our destiny, God will on many occasions cut off the manna supply to push us to the next level of having more than enough!

I challenge you to break free from the world system and walk in divine provision! Our Lord taught us to pray that the Father's Kingdom come and that His will be done. Therefore;

1.   We must take our dominion and reign.

2.   We must tap into supernatural resources to accomplish God's purpose.

3.   We should take possession of all that is legally ours according to the Word of God.

4.   We must bring down into the physical what is already ours in the spiritual realm.

5.   We must break free from the wilderness mentality and possess our Canaan.

Andrew Mutana

6.   We must risk moving out of the comfort zone to this level of abundance.

7.   We cannot keep doing the same things and expect to achieve different results. Nor can we break free from a legacy of failure, defeat and poverty handed down to us by our fathers unless we do something they never did.

CHAPTER 25

I DARE YOU TO GET OUT OF THAT WOMB!

When a baby reaches his or her 9 months' full term in the mother's womb, he or she must come out. Birth is another time of transition. Every transition is uncomfortable. Temperatures are not regulated; sickness, pain and pollution are some of the things this baby will have to face.

However, babies are not meant to stay inside the womb. When they stay longer than the gestation period, something is wrong. When they come out early, still something is terribly wrong. In this case they need to be prepared more for the new life outside.

When the delivery time comes and the water bag bursts, the contractions in the mother's womb cause the baby to be pushed out. When it comes out, the first thing will be to sever the link to the mother (umbilical cord). This means that this baby must adjust to a new way of life.

When the Israelites crossed into the Promised Land the manna ceased immediately. God knew that this generation was ready to fight and take the promises.

They had to move to the next level of accessing the promises they had heard since they were in Egypt.

Our God is a rich God. As a wealthy family prepares adequately for an expected baby, so does He for all of us. Some families even have a separate bank account for this child before he/she is born that would cater for all their needs through school.

As your faith is, so your life shall be!

As money is to the worldly system, faith is the currency we need for exchange in the Kingdom.

As we grow in the knowledge and understanding of His ways, we begin to discover the exceeding greatness of His riches (Ephesians 1: 18-20).

God told Moses to send spies into Canaan. When they came back, they all had different reports. They saw the same land but interpreted it differently. They all carried of the fruit of the land and testified that it was indeed a land flowing with milk and honey.

The problem is that one group was not prepared to fight for their inheritance. They didn't have the passion to carry them through the suffering of the wilderness to the promise. They didn't see things with the eyes of faith. They concentrated on the giants (sons of Anak) and could no longer see the power of God.

Just imagine a God who had divided the Red Sea before their eyes! He also gave them water out of rocks and did many mighty and fearful miracles in Egypt.

Before we judge them harshly, let me quickly suggest that we live our lives like them most of the time. Though we profess to believe, we are non-believing believers. We keep moving from defeat to defeat. We spend our lives surviving instead of living and making an impact.

We have talked so much about the generation curse in the church. It is not enough, though, to break the generation curse. We must walk in the generation blessing. The curse only goes to four generations but the blessing goes up to one thousand generations!

God has more than enough for your vision!

Deuteronomy 8:3:

And he humbled thee, and suffered thee to hunger, and fed thee with manna, which thou knewest not, nor did thy fathers know; that he might make thee know that man doth not live by bread only, but by every word that proceedeth out of the mouth of the Lord doth man live.

God took the Israelites through the wilderness and humbled them in order that that they would understand this truth. Bread talks of natural means; means that which can be seen. Faith has to do with the unseen, the unlimited and the supernatural.

It is God's desire and design that His church will live by faith (the just shall live by faith). The Kingdom of God is only accessed by faith.

When the scripture talks of every word, it brings us back to Genesis 1:1. The Word God spoke caused things to be created from the unseen. From nothing, the whole world was created, as we know it. By faith even worlds that we don't know yet were created.

Is God your source?

The economies of the world are being shaken. The price of oil is escalating. Many stock markets will fail to sustain the failing economies. Many life savings will be wiped out. The world is being prepared for the cashless society.

God is however also training His people to look to Him as their source. Jesus talked of keeping our treasure in heaven where moth, rust and decay cannot corrupt it. It is only those that have learnt to tap in divine provision that will survive the bad times. They will even continue to prosper and increase.

There are several ways in which God is training His people to depend on Him and to secure their financial future.

1- We must faithfully pay our tithes and offerings. This takes away the curse as we read in Malachi 3:10. God also rebukes the devourer on our behalf.

2- We must listen to God concerning sowing our finances into the Kingdom of God and into His purposes. The world teaches us to keep for ourselves as much as possible. Kingdom economics however teaches that he who sows sparingly shall also reap sparingly. (2 Corinthians 9:6)

The Gospel has to be preached. God will transfer wealth into the hand of men and women who are willing to release it into His work and not consume it on their fleshly lusts.

3-   We must also hear from God on how to save and invest. This means we also must research from the natural source before investing and consult the experts who know the market well. Solomon advises in Proverbs that there is safety in a multitude of counselors.

You will not lack in Jesus name!

When we realize our potential and walk in our divine destiny, we stop running after provision. Provision is meant to overtake the vision. All this will happen automatically as we maximize the entire God given potential within us. Our attitude should be to make use of every opportunity to gain wealth. There is no limit to our blessing and prosperity. We know that prosperity is more than having a lot of money. It is really living a full life.

To walk in divine provision, we must move away from dependence on natural means and sources to tapping into God's inexhaustible resources. Isn't it time you and I stopped looking to our employers, business or vocation as our source? All these natural means can and will be shaken. God alone cannot be shaken and in Him should our trust be.

•   God will make all grace abound to us that we will have all sufficiency in all things. He is raising a standard of a people that He will use to finance the end time revival. (2 Corinthians 9:8)

• In Hebrews, we are told that we have received a Kingdom that cannot be shaken. (Hebrews 12:28) Regardless of the state of national or world economies, God's purpose will stand.

• His will is that we get blessed. And it is only His blessing that makes rich and He adds no sorrow with it. (Proverbs 10:22) What confuses many is the fact that there are stages that we must go through to enjoy this prosperity. Remember, 3 John 2 says that we only prosper as our souls prosper. Yet, we often expect to see instant prosperity and increase. If it is from God, then we have to get it His way. We cannot bow down to the system of the world and expect to walk in divine blessing.

• Every word of God is likened to silver tried seven times. This means that we have to be willing to suffer pain as this word is purified. When we quit under pressure we miss the benefits of the Word and our breakthrough. God's desire is that each level we leave we must never get back.

God is stirring a remnant that is going to influence the world in a major way – in every sphere and aspect of life. For this to happen the church has to start to hear God. Each of us must walk in His perfect will for our lives.

As is often said, "God will never take us from glory to grass". You will stop pursuing things but allow things to pursue you!

You will have dominion over things that now have dominion over you in Jesus name!

Part VII

Power

But you shall [earnestly] remember the Lord your God, for it is He who gives you power to get wealth, that He may establish His covenant which He swore to your fathers, as it is this day.

Deuteronomy 8:18 (Amplified Version)

Andrew Mutana

CHAPTER 26

POWER

*E*phesians 3:20:

Now unto Him that is able to do e ceeding abundantly above all that we ask or think, according to the power that worketh in us.

Romans 8:28:

And we know that all things work together for good to them that love God, to them who are called according to His purpose.

God is able to make you what He wants you to be. To Him belongs the power. He will give us the power to ful ll His purposes for our lives.

Yes, according to Ephesians 3:20, all this power is at work in your life and in my life! He is able to exceed our expectations and wildest imaginations. He can do much more than we could ever ask or pray for.

You don't have to worry or be intimidated by the gap between your vision and the reality of your circumstances. He will give you favor and the right connections with the people you need. He will also open the doors for you that you need to walk through.

I am persuaded and convinced of His power at work in my life. You should too. Why?

1.   God has already written His plan for our lives

He has the power to change our present circumstances, redeem our broken past and give us our dream future – His purpose for our lives is in Jeremiah 29:11.

In Psalm 40:7, David speaks prophetically;

Then said I, Lo, I come: in the volume of the book it is written of me.

It is clear that David here was not just talking about himself but also of the Messiah who was to come. However, I also believe that this scripture applies to you and me. God has huge volume. All of our days are contained in this book.

Nothing will ever happen to us that will take Him by surprise. In fact, nothing just happens to us once we give our lives over to Him. All our steps are ordered. Once I realized this, I rested. He knows me better than I know myself. And He cares.

2.   We are original

One day, I was reading a tiny book by Dr. T.L Osborn entitled "You are God's best". He wrote certain things that spoke directly to me. One of the statements I remember is; "God never created a second hand; you are first class; you were created to accomplish something that nobody else can ever accomplish."

There is tremendous power in originality. It carries an anointing that breaks the back of the enemy and ushers us into our destiny in God. However, as we saw earlier, for us to become original and authentic we must be willing to go through God's process.

When we emerge out of God's process, we are a voice and not an echo. We are not imitations. Nor do we walk as another man's shadow.

We are real and authentic. We do not need any man's commendation or attestation. We have a message, a testimony and an experience. God attests to the fact that we are His chosen by the anointing He imparts to us. This anointing enables us to break through the mould.

3. As we walk in our purpose, we have the passion to accomplish our mandate

Power always follows passion. Passion is only ignited by purpose. It is that power that keeps you moving when you cannot move anymore; that inner strength that we draw on to keep on keeping on. It is the power that drives us to the next level. It is like the marathon runner who feels totally exhausted but sees the finish line a few meters away. It is said that they draw on some strength to make it to the end. Allow me to say that it is passion that determines who wins the race.

4. We are born of God

John 5:4 says that whatever is born of God overcomes the world. There is a process that God has designed for you to take you where He wants you to be. Nothing, nobody, not even the devil and all his demons combined can stop you from getting to your destiny.

However, it is important to keep focused on the prize to avoid delaying or stopping our destiny. It is only you and I that have the power to stop God's purpose.

For example, Abraham had a promise from God to be a father of many nations through his son Isaac. When he allowed himself to be distracted from the process, he produced Ishmael.

Don't fall into that trap. Wait on God!

Most of the things in your destiny are in His control. Keep your hope in Him. Don't worry about how it will all work out. Because you are His child, you will overcome.

Greater is He who is in us than the devil that is in the world! (1 John 4:4)

CHAPTER 27

FINAL THOUGHTS

As I finish this book, I would like to point out certain things that you must accept, embrace and walk in to see your destiny come to pass.

• You are created in the image of God. Accept your uniqueness. Your uniqueness is your greatest asset. Until you become original you can never be authentic.

• You are designed for a purpose and destiny like none other. Celebrate yourself. There will be times when no one seems to stand with you. Be confident in the fact that God will always stand with you. Hold your head high. As Paul told Timothy, "Don't let anyone look down on you..." For Timothy, it was because of his age. In fact, nobody has any reason or the right to look down on you.

• Everything in your past has been designed and orchestrated by a divine invisible hand to direct your life in its course. Stop blaming people in your life for what they did or didn't do. God has enough power to turnaround the bad things for His purpose. Your pain is what qualifies you to help anybody – it is your ministry. No other person can have your testimony. Therefore, no other person can minister to the world the way you can.

- There is enough power within you to be all that you are supposed to be. Nobody needs to believe in your dream for it to come to pass. Stop focusing on who doesn't like you but instead see all the blessings you have. Believe in yourself every single day.

- You can never walk into your destiny still holding to your past. You must let go and let God.

- Your best days are not behind you. They are ahead of you.

- Make the most of what you have instead of complaining about what you don't have. When God was sending Moses to his assignment, He asked him, "What do you have in your hand?" It is not about what you don't have; it is what you have that God will use to take you where you have not been. You have your place, your garden, your blessing, your miracle and breakthrough – with your name on it!

- Celebrate others. Help them achieve their destiny as much as possible. I learnt this from my pastor; "What you make happen for others, God will make happen for you!" The more you rejoice in other's success, pray and help them; the faster will be your own breakthrough.

- Sow seeds. Everything on earth operates on the principle of seedtime and harvest. Whatever a man sows, that shall he also reap (Galatians 6:7).

What stirred me to write this book is the knowledge that there are so many people out there with great potential. The world has told them that they cannot make it.

But if God can get me from all the things He has got me from, then He sure can help you too.

If you don't have a personal relationship with Him, you should. He will change your life and bring meaning to it – as you had never dreamt possible. He did to mine!

Discovering God's purpose and your destiny will help you live a fulfilled and satisfied life. God bless you as you listen to His voice.

Begin to move in the direction He has planned for your life!

-The End-

Spiritual Warfare

In 2006, Pastor Mutana asked several believers to accompany him to pray for a woman who had unknowingly exposed herself to the demonic and occult world. Most of the believers were afraid of getting involved, and Pastor Mutana realized that most children of God don't know how to exercise authority over the enemy. In this book, you will learn:

1. That Satan's chief weapons are lies and fear

2. How to pray with authority

3. That Jesus is a man of war - more powerful than most of us imagine

Living on the Edge of a Miracle

In this book, Pastor Mutana shares his journey of faith, telling of how he walked away from a promising Engineering career into full time ministry. In this book you will learn:

1. How to rely on revelation and not just on information

2. How to exercise faith for your healing

3. About God's desire for you to be completely debt free

Upsetting The Status Quo

Revival is a revolution!

Shall we have:

Revival or ruin?

Christ or chaos?

Fire of renewal or judgment?

This book is a prophetic call. It is sounding the alarm. It is a must read for all those who are sick and tired of the enemies work against our families, nations and lives.

ABOUT THE AUTHOR

Andrew Mutana is an ordained minister. He trained professionally as an Electrical Engineer. He resigned in 2003 and has been full-time in ministry since. Over this period, he has led mission teams to over 20 countries around the world.

He is the pastor of Impact Church - a growing vibrant church in the Westlands area of Nairobi, Kenya.

He is the author of 5 books: Upsetting the Status quo, Spiritual Warfare, Living on the edge of a miracle, Destiny Pursuers and Prayer power (His latest). Two books can be purchased on Amazon.

He also has a passion for praise and worship. He has written many songs.

He is married to Deborah and they have six amazing children.

He is married to Deborah and they have six amazing children.

www.impactchurch.co.ke

facebook: Impactchurchke

Twitter: Impactchurchke1/Andrewmutana

Instagram: Impactchurchke1

Youtube: impactchurch/Andrew Mutana (Please subscribe!)

Thanks for reading! Please add a short review on Amazon and let me know what you thought!

Andrew Mutana